SLOVIN V. SLOVIN

SECOND EDITION

SLOVIN V. SLOVIN

SECOND EDITION

Barbara S. Barron

Professor of Skills
Maurice A. Deane School of Law
at Hofstra University

Lawrence W. Kessler

Richard J. Cardali Distinguished Professor of Trial Advocacy
Maurice A. Deane School of Law
at Hofstra University

NATIONAL INSTITUTE FOR TRIAL ADVOCACY

Address inquiries to:

Reprint Permission
National Institute for Trial Advocacy
1685 38th Street, Suite 200
Boulder, CO 80301-2735
Phone: (800) 225-6482
Fax: (720) 890-7069
Email: permissions@nita.org

ISBN 978-1-60156-481-8
eISBN 978-1-60156-517-4
FBA 1481

Printed in the United States of America

CONTENTS

INTRODUCTION

This is a multifaceted matrimonial action. As with most matrimonial actions, the filing for divorce created a cascade of related litigations concerning matrimonial torts, distribution of property, and the custody of the children.

The litigation started when Rita Slovin sued her husband, Michael Slovin, for divorce under the jurisdiction's no-fault divorce provisions. Ms. Slovin seeks sole custody of the couple's two children. Mr. Slovin seeks a significant equitable distribution award and also requests sole custody of the two children. Additionally, Mr. Slovin has brought a separate action against Ms. Slovin for battery and slander.

The case file is a multi-purpose one. It can be used as a trial/litigation skills tool for developing expertise in trying equitable distribution and child custody claims with a focus on expert testimony. Equitable distribution[1] and child custody claims equally and easily form the basis of negotiation exercises. The first two modules focus on child custody—the negotiation and trial of the child custody case. The second two modules concern the trial and negotiation of financial issues, with sole consideration to equitable distribution. In addition to those traditional matrimonial litigation issues, there is an additional module that introduces the theory of marital tort as an offshoot of the matrimonial litigation. There are two causes of action, one for battery and the other for defamation. The insertion of those two tort claims allows for additional training in basic trial advocacy skills while developing more complex theories of the case. Further, the related battery and defamation actions allow participants to gradually develop their advocacy skills. The battery claim is a simple action, while the slander claim is more complex because of the various affirmative defenses.

Note: Each module may be used as a stand-alone case file. The specific party and witness statements that appear in a particular module have been designed to fit the theoretical, strategic, and tactical goals of the litigation or negotiation exercise. Therefore, the statements in one module may not be identical to the statements in another module. The specific problems that appear at the end of this case file will relate to the particular module and the particular witness statements contained therein.

The order of the modules is as follows:

Module 1: Trying the Child Custody Case

Module 2: Negotiating the Child Custody Case

Module 3: Trying the Equitable Distribution Case

Module 4: Negotiating the Equitable Distribution Case

---

1. Please note that the purpose of the equitable distribution claims is to develop the trainee's basic ability to examine experts persuasively to support the client's claims. It is *not* to develop advanced expertise in the highly technical area of forensic accounting theories vis-à-vis the complex world of equitable distribution of the marital estate. As a result, the formulas, theories, and calculations used in the case file have been designed to allow for easy understanding and analysis that will translate into persuasive advocacy presentations. They may not conform to the reality of financial forensic accounting principles in analyzing and determining equitable distribution claims.

Module 5: Trying the Marital Torts—Battery and Defamation

All years in the materials are stated in the following form:

YR-0 indicates the actual year in which the case is being tried (i.e., the present year);

YR-1 indicates the next preceding year (please use the actual year);

YR-2 indicates the second preceding year (please use the actual year), etc.

SUPREME COURT OF THE STATE OF NITA
COUNTY OF DARROW COUNTY

Rita Slovin,	)	Index No.:
Plaintiff,	)	
	)	
against	)	**VERIFIED COMPLAINT**
	)	**ACTION FOR DIVORCE**
Michael Slovin,	)	
Defendant.	)	

<u>VERIFIED COMPLAINT</u>

1. The plaintiff, Rita Slovin, complaining of the defendant, Michael Slovin, alleges that the parties are over the age of eighteen years.

2. The plaintiff and the defendant have resided in Nita for a continuous period of at least two years immediately preceding the commencement of this divorce action.

3. The plaintiff and the defendant were married on November 18, YR-10, in Nita City, Nita.

4. The marriage was not performed by a clergyman, minister, or by a leader of the Society for Ethical Culture.

5. The plaintiff will take prior to the entry of final judgment all steps solely within her power to the best of her knowledge to remove any barrier to the defendant's remarriage.

6. There are two children of the marriage.

Name	Date of Birth	Address
Loren Slovin	YR-10	400 Schoolhouse Lane, Nita City, Nita
Sasha Slovin	YR-6	400 Schoolhouse Lane, Nita City, Nita

    The plaintiff resides at 400 Schoolhouse Lane, Nita City. The defendant resides at 92-08 Bellage Boulevard, Nita City.

7. The grounds for divorce that are alleged as follows:

    That the relationship between the plaintiff and the defendant has broken down irretrievably for a period of at least six months.

8. There is no judgment of divorce and no other matrimonial action between the parties pending in this court or in any other court of competent jurisdiction.

WHEREFORE, the plaintiff demands judgment against the defendant:

1. Divorcing the parties hereto and dissolving the marital relationship heretofore existing between them;

2. Awarding the plaintiff sole custody of the minor children of the parties;

3. Awarding the plaintiff child support in accordance with the laws of Nita;

4. Awarding the plaintiff spousal support in accordance with the laws of Nita:

5. Awarding the plaintiff sole occupancy of the marital residence;

6. Awarding the plaintiff equitable distribution of marital property;

7. Declaring the plaintiff's separate property; and

8. Awarding the plaintiff such other and further relief as this Court deems fit and proper.

Dated: December 16, YR-2

Lenora Wilder

Forest Green
Nyman and Seymour

By: Lenora Wilder
Attorney Number: 867590

Attorneys for Plaintiff
1966 Broadway #1219
Nita City, Nita 09999

STATE OF NITA   ))
ss:))
COUNTY OF DARROW   ))
_____

I, Rita Slovin, am the plaintiff in the within action for a divorce. I have read the foregoing complaint and know the contents thereof. The contents are true to my own knowledge except as to matters therein stated to be alleged upon information and belief and as to those matters I believe them to be true.

                              Subscribed and sworn to
                              before me this 16th day of December, YR-2

                              Rita Slovin
                              _____
                              Rita Slovin

                              Harry Struck
                              _____
                              Notary Public for the State of Nita

SUPREME COURT OF THE STATE OF NITA
COUNTY OF DARROW COUNTY

Rita Slovin, Plaintiff,	)))	Index No.:
against	))	**VERIFIED ANSWER** **ACTION FOR DIVORCE**
Michael Slovin, Defendant.	))	

VERIFIED ANSWER

The defendant, Michael Slovin, by his attorney, answers the allegations in the plaintiff's verified complaint, as follows:

1. Admits the allegations in ¶¶ 1, 2, 3, 4, 6, and 8 of the plaintiff's verified complaint.

2. Denies knowledge or information sufficient to form a belief as to the truth of the allegations in ¶ 5 of the plaintiff's verified complaint.

3. Denies each and every allegation set forth in ¶ 7 of the plaintiff's verified complaint.

WHEREFORE, the defendant demands judgment against the plaintiff:

1. Awarding the defendant sole custody of the minor children of the parties;

2. Awarding the defendant child support in accordance with the laws of Nita;

3. Awarding the defendant spousal support for the lifetime of the defendant in an amount in accordance with the laws of Nita;

4. Awarding the defendant an equitable distribution of the marital property;

5. Directing the plaintiff to maintain adequate medical insurance for the benefit of the defendant and the minor children of the marriage;

6. Directing the plaintiff to maintain adequate life insurance for the benefit of the defendant and the minor children of the marriage;

7. Directing the plaintiff to contribute to the defendant's counsel fees and litigation expenses; and

8. Awarding the defendant any other and further relief this Court deems fit and proper.

Attorney for Defendant
Dated: January 8, YR-1

Arthur Kaufman
_____

Arthur Kaufman
Arthur Kaufman & Associates
510 26th Avenue
Nita City, Nita 09999

STATE OF NITA   ))
ss   ))
COUNTY OF DARROW   ))

I, Michael Slovin, am the defendant in the within action for a divorce. I have read the foregoing complaint and know the contents thereof. The contents are true to my own knowledge except as to matters therein stated to be alleged upon information and belief and as to those matters I believe them to be true.

Subscribed and sworn to
before me on this 8th day of January, YR-1

Michael Slovin
_____
Michael Slovin

Harry Struck
_____
Notary Public for the State of Nita

Module 1

Trying the Child Custody Case

SUPREME COURT OF THE STATE OF NITA
COUNTY OF DARROW COUNTY

Rita Slovin,   )   Index No.:
Plaintiff,   )
)
against   )   **MEMORANDUM ORDER GRANTING**
)   **A HEARING ON CHILD CUSTODY**
Michael Slovin,   )
Defendant.   )

Dearborn, J.

MEMORANDUM AND ORDER

This is a matrimonial action. The defendant, Michael Slovin, has moved for an order granting him sole custody of the infant issue of the subject marriage. The plaintiff, Rita Slovin, has cross-moved for an order granting sole custody of the infant issue of the subject marriage. Because of the complicated issues addressed in the parties' respective motions, a summary grant or denial of the respective motions is inappropriate. Those issues warrant a full hearing before a fact finder.

IT IS HEREBY ORDERED that a full hearing and trial be held on the following issues:

1. Whether the defendant, Michael Slovin, should be granted full custody of the infant children of the marriage, Loren and Sasha Slovin;

2. Whether the plaintiff, Rita Slovin, should be granted full custody of the infant children of the marriage, Loren and Sasha Slovin; in the alternative;

3. Whether the defendant, Michael Slovin, should be granted sole physical custody of the infant children of the marriage, Loren and Sasha Slovin, and joint decision-making authority with the plaintiff, Rita Slovin;

4. Whether the plaintiff, Rita Slovin, should be granted sole physical custody of the infant children of the marriage, Loren and Sasha Slovin, and joint decision-making authority with the defendant, Michael Slovin; and

5. Whether the parties should be granted joint physical custody of and joint decision-making authority over the infant children of the marriage, Loren and Sasha Slovin.

SO ORDERED:

Dated: January 12, YR-0

Carlos Dearborn

Carlos Dearborn

CORE DOCTRINAL CONCEPTS CONCERNING CHILD CUSTODY

Definitions—Child Custody

1. In any action or proceeding brought for a divorce, the court shall enter orders for custody and support as, in the court's discretion, justice requires, having regard to the circumstances of the case and of the respective parties and to the best interests of the child.

2. There is no prima facie right to custody. Either parent may be awarded custody of the child. There are no set factors by which a court may determine custody. It is up to the court, given the particular circumstances of the case; the parties; and the needs of the child.

3. A custodial parent who is awarded "physical custody" of a child or children pursuant to a valid agreement between the parties or by an order or decree of a court shall have the child or children permanently and they shall legally reside with that parent.

4. A parent who is awarded "decision-making authority" of a child or children pursuant to a valid agreement between the parties or by an order or decree of a court shall have the ability to make decisions regarding the health, education, and welfare of the child or children. A court may award decision-making authority to either or both parents. A parent does not have to be the "custodial parent" to be awarded decision-making authority.

5. "Joint Physical Custody" means that both parents have a shared legal right to reside with the children.

STATEMENT OF MICHAEL SLOVIN

1   I am thirty-nine years old. I have a PhD in special education from Nita University. I got the

2   doctorate in YR-10. I also have both a BS and an MS in psychology from Nita University.

3   I went to Choate and Brown before that. I met Rita at school in YR-11. She was in college.

4   She graduated in YR-10. We were married in YR-10, during the spring semester. She and

5   I got our degrees a few months after the marriage. I worked as a special education teacher

6   after we were married. I made a salary of $30,000 per year from YR-10 until YR-9. Rita

7   started working in her family's business as soon as she got out of college. She always made

8   a very good salary (up to $200,000 in YR-1) and got an annual shareholder's distribution of

9    $100,000 as well. She has a minor job in the company but is well paid because she owns it.

10   Her draw of profits is small because of the terms of the partnership agreement. That agree-

11   ment contains a provision in which she said, "I was really getting more than I should in light

12   of how much my brother George does and how little I do." She has always said this about

13   her role. I am sure she could have gotten a bigger draw if her work was more important to

14   the company's success.

15

16   I stopped working full time a year after Loren was born (December 8, YR-10) so that I could

17   be at home and give the baby the nurturing she needed. I spent all of my time with Loren.

18   In YR-8, we moved into a new house, at 400 Schoolhouse Lane, Nita City, Nita, that was big

19   enough for children.

20

21   We bought the house for $1 million. Rita borrowed the money from the company. George

22   gave her a 1 percent loan. When she got the money, she put it into our joint bank account. We

23   have paid all of the expenses of maintaining the house with our joint money. The new roof,

24   the taxes, the plumbing, the decorating expenses all came from our joint money. Rita now

25   says that she didn't borrow the money. I know she did. I even have a copy of the loan agree-

26   ment. I don't know where the signed one is. It used to be in with our papers. The last time

27   I looked it was gone. The copy I have was one that I put with my patient notes by accident.

28   I guess that it would be gone, too, if anyone had known where it was.

1   Loren and I had a wonderful time. I had been raised by nannies, as my parents spent a lot of

2   time traveling. I was then sent to boarding school. I didn't want the same type of childhood

3   for my children.

4

5   Things between me and Rita changed when I stayed at home. The most obvious change

6   occurred because Rita didn't think that I spent enough time doing housework. I told her that

7   I was a parent and that she had plenty of money to hire a maid if she didn't like the way I made

8   the beds. Rita hired Linda Allen a year after we moved into the new house. She was hired in

9   November YR-7. After that, I was able to spend a little time on myself. I am a very good tennis

10   player, and I play frequently. I have played in Bookerman's "A" Singles and Doubles leagues

11   since YR-5. At my age, I find that I have to work to stay in shape, so I go to the gym several times

12   a week. In YR-7, I started taking Chinese and guitar lessons. I get great pleasure out of both.

13   After a few years, I acquired some skill and, therefore, for the last three years I have belonged

14   to a Chinese discussion group and a guitar orchestra. Each meets one evening per week.

15

16   I started working part time shortly after Sasha was born, in November YR-6. I started a consulting

17   business (Special Needs R Us) for physically and developmentally disabled children. Before Rita

18   and I separated, I carried about a ten-patient load and earned no more than $25,000. I spend

19   approximately eleven to twelve hours per week working. I have had to turn down many patients

20   and several consulting arrangements because the time commitment that work would have

21   required would have prevented me from performing my primary job, which has been parenting.

22

23   The primary focus of my life was still the children. I spent at least an hour with the children after

24   supper. I put them to bed every weekday night, except for the orchestra and discussion group

25   evenings. I also cooked with them when Linda wasn't there. Almost every week, I took the kids on

26   a trip. The zoo and the natural history museum are favorites. Rita went along some of the time.

27

28   While Linda Allen worked for Rita, she and I dressed, fed, and supervised the children. I told

29   her what to do, and Linda did it. I told her what clothing to select. She then would get the

30   clothing and dress them.

1   Rita does not understand the kids' needs. She is so committed to her business that she doesn't

2   have time for them. Her major concern is that the children should not interfere with her quiet

3   respite at home. She is the kind of perfectionist who kills enjoyment in life. For example,

4   she insists that everything be in its exact place, at all times. When Loren was a baby, Rita

5   constantly complained if I waited fifteen minutes before changing Loren's diaper or didn't

6   wash the dishes right after the meal was over. The kids' toys have to be put away before they

7   finish playing. As soon as one toy isn't being touched, she wants it put away. As a result of

8   this obsession, she frequently called me a "freeloader" or a "slob" in their presence. She has

9   abused me in front of the children and often has yelled at me in front of them. It wasn't so

10   bad when they were young, but now they understand. On the weekends, when Linda was off,

11   Rita used to run the house like a hotel. She washed everything, put everything away, orga-

12   nized all the toys, and generally made it impossible for me to tolerate her. After Sasha was

13   born, I would just leave the house on Saturday and Sunday mornings and stay out the entire

14   day. It was a respite from her control and from my home responsibilities.

15

16   Because of her singular focus on herself, she is a martinet and that makes for a very bad

17   mother. I often have to remind her of the fact that they need her or she would never spend

18   any time with them. I have tried to keep them from being upset by the little attention that

19   she chooses to give to them. I have explained that it is just her way; that she loves them, but

20   is too busy to show it; that some people are less sensitive about the feelings of others; that

21   learning how to deal with her will be good training for the difficult people they will confront

22   at school and later in life.

23

24   The worst episode with Rita occurred just after Loren's eighth birthday. That is Rita's busiest

25   time of the year. After allegedly sleeping on the couch in her office, she came home an hour

26   after she had told us she would. When she waltzed in, I quietly told her that the children were

27   upset by having to wait for her and I had put them to bed. She started shouting at me. She

28   said that I was trying to poison the children against her. She screamed that I was just living off

29   her money and using the kids as an excuse to live the life of a bum. I tried to calm her down.

30   But the more I told her that we loved her the best we could, the more I told her that it was the

1   strain of her being away so much that was causing the problems, the more out of control she

2   got. I think that Loren heard us. I know that Rita called me a "bum" and a "disgusting whore"

3   and "the perfect 1950s wife." She stormed out of the room with the line, "I thought I married

4   a man, but I seem to have gotten an expensive *au pair*."

5

6   My relationship with Rita has not been good. For example, we haven't had sex since YR-3.

7   I think that she is having an affair with Tommy Friel. I know that he has a male boyfriend, but

8   that doesn't mean that he can't have sex with women. For the last two years of our marriage,

9   he has been coming to the house every morning and coming home with her every night. They

10   always work the same hours, often until 11:00 p.m. I am sure that he was with her when she

11   didn't come home after Loren's eighth birthday. I haven't seen them, but I am sure that they

12   stopped off for some "quiet time" together on some of those late nights.

13

14   As the years passed, I became more and more dissatisfied with my marriage. I was thinking of

15   leaving. I couldn't take it anymore and on December 16, YR-2, I left.

16

17   It was a very tense time. The night before, Rita had told me something about quitting her job.

18   I don't remember exactly what she said on the evening of December 15, YR-2, but I didn't

19   believe it for a second. I have been trying to get her to quit or slow down for years. She com-

20   plained endlessly about the long hours, but it was obvious that she loved the job more than

21   she loved her family. She never would have quit.

22

23   When I left Rita's house on December 16, YR-2, I moved to 92-08 Bellage Boulevard, Nita City.

24   Linda and I and the kids live there. My father owns the house. I picked the Bellage Boulevard

25   residence so that the children would be able to stay in the same school and see their mother.

26   I was able to buy the house from my father because he gave me a purchase money mortgage.

27   He has also helped me with money to furnish the place.

28

29   Linda helped me take the children and formally moved in a few months later. Linda Allen

30   and I had no intimate physical relationship before my separation from Rita. Of course, when

1   the kids stay with me, she stays, too. That is because she lives here. Now, of course, we are

2   emotionally and physically intimate. I have had nurturing and protective feelings about Linda

3   for a long time. Even before we started living together, I wanted to support her in any way

4   I could. On several occasions, I let her sleep in the huge bedroom bed at 400 Schoolhouse

5   Lane because she was emotionally distressed and I didn't think that it was appropriate for her

6   to be alone until she felt more secure, so she did sleep there once or twice. But there were

7   no intimacies. I just let her sleep in my room to protect and calm her. If Rita was in the house

8   and Linda was distraught, I would sit with her in her room until she was asleep.

9

10 Linda is such a wonderful person that her joy radiates. As a result, I have long enjoyed giving

11 her presents as much to see how happy they made her as to thank her for the way she nur-

12 tured the children. One gift was a little over the top. It was a birthday gift of a diamond and

13 ruby necklace that cost $1,500. I never specifically told Rita about my gift to Linda because

14 it was a gift from me, not Rita and me. Rita must have known, however, because Linda wore

15 the necklace all the time. Later, I heard that she claimed to have been shocked to learn about

16 my gift. I doubt if she was shocked, but I was shocked when I heard that she told blatant lies

17 about me to several of our joint friends, my new employer, and many others.

18

19 Although Linda and I live together, we are very careful to avoid being intimate in the presence

20 of the children. I have kissed and held her in their presence. In fact, we were just kissing when

21 Rita walked in to pick up the kids on March 15, YR-1. We were on the couch in the family room

22 while the kids were watching a DVD in front of us. Rita's story that we were acting improperly

23 is absurd. Linda had just taken a shower, and we were just lying together watching TV while

24 waiting for Rita to come and pick up the kids.

25

26 I am presently self-employed as a consultant, and I also have a private therapy practice.

27 Since Rita and I separated, I have worked hard to expand my practice. This has taken me

28 away from the children, but I have been earning a little more than $40,000 a year from my

29 consulting and therapy practice. I have gotten a job offer in Aba, Nita. I have arranged to

30 commute from my home so that the children will not be removed from their friends and

1   from the opportunity to visit their mother. I will make $155,000 a year supervising a research

2   project on child disabilities for the Everflash Institute. It is a great opportunity for me. I expect

3   that my income will exceed $250,000 during the two years of the grant that will support the

4   research project because I will be able to continue my consulting business as well. In fact, this

5   significant position with Everflash will lead to a much more robust private practice, since a

6   psychologist's business directly relates to his reputation.

7

8   I left Rita because I just couldn't take her abuse and the flaunting of her relationship with

9   Friel. On December 16, YR-2, he stopped by for his usual ride to work. The two of them were

10   standing at the door giggling at each other. Linda was dressing the children in their rooms.

11   I accused them of having an affair. The way they were acting was just rubbing my nose in it.

12   Rita, of course, denied it. Tommy just stood there looking guilty. When she said that I was

13   crazy, I couldn't take it anymore. We shouted at each other for about two minutes. I was

14   standing near the kitchen, and she was facing me on the other side of the hallway. I started to

15   walk away from her to go to the kitchen. Rita moved in front of me and pushed me very hard

16   so that I was thrust into the wall.

17

18   At that point, I saw that the children were watching from the top of the stairs. There is a little

19   balcony, and they were standing along the rail. I told Rita to get out. She told me that she had

20   bought the house and that if anyone was leaving it was me. I left. Linda packed our things, and

21   I carried them to the car. I wanted to get out as fast as I could. I did not say anything because

22   I did not want to worry Linda or the kids, but my arm was throbbing so much that I had trouble

23   holding the heavy bags. I dropped one down a whole flight of stairs.

24

25   Linda and I had been planning to have lunch at The Homestead. Linda had packed up things

26   for the children's day. I had asked Linda to get the kids' things ready so that she wouldn't be

27   delayed in going to eat.

28

29   Rita is now trying to destroy my business. In February YR-1, I started to build up my practice

30   so that I had ten regular patients, each of whom saw me once or twice a week, in addition to

1   my work for Everflash. By the end of YR-1, all but one of those patients had left me. The loss

2   of patients is, of course, normal, as people recover. However, I have been unable to replace

3   them because of the terrible lies that Rita has been spreading about me. She is very sick, and

4   in her condition it would not be right to get her involved.

5

6   It is her proclivity to act in this kind of malevolent manner that causes me to insist on having

7   the sole rights of decision making and legal custody to protect the children.

STATEMENT OF RITA SLOVIN

1   I am now thirty-three years old. I met Michael while I was in college. He was a lot older than I,

2   and was getting a graduate degree. He was a teaching assistant in my psychology class. We hit

3   it off immediately. He was very understanding. He seemed so mature and caring. We dated

4   for two years and got married immediately before I graduated in YR-10.

5

6   Before he died, my father built a very successful business that he called Perfect Toys. He initially

7   manufactured seasonal toys and notions. After a while, however, United States manufacturing

8   costs became too high and he manufactured abroad. When he died in January of YR-10, the

9   business was valued at $10 million. My brother George, who is fifteen years older than I am,

10   took over. George has done a wonderful job. The value of the company is now about $20 million.

11

12   The company's management consists of my brother George, who is president; my mother

13   Sylvia, who is vice president and secretary; and me. I am treasurer. I have a twenty-five

14   percent interest in the company. My mother has a forty percent interest, and George has

15   a thirty-five percent interest. Those percentage interests were not our idea. My father had

16   come up with the percentages before he died. He did not want anyone to have a major-

17   ity interest. He each left us a portion of the company in his will and instructed his lawyers

18   to draft a shareholder's agreement and a stock purchase agreement, which set forth each

19   owner's interest and value of each share, respectively.

20

21   I do not see any of that corporate income, other than a $100,000 annual draw. The rest

22   just appears on my return pursuant to IRS regulations. That is what our accountants tell me.

23   I know that not one penny of the company's earnings, other than the salary I draw as head

24   of collections, gets into my bank account. I earn $200,000 a year. I have a title as head of our

25   collections department. The shareholder's agreement we signed when I became of age gave

26   each of us the right to renegotiate profit distribution terms every ten years. I couldn't ask for

27   more money, however, because I just don't do that much.

1   My job has been to collect money from recalcitrant purchasers. Although collecting money is

2   important, the total amount has never more than five percent of our gross in any year. I am

3   overpaid for my work. I am sure it is because I am the boss's sister. The reason I do not have

4   to do much as collections head is that my brother has supplied me with a fabulous team of

5   managers. They keep meticulous computerized records of our accounts. Our customers gener-

6   ally pay on time, which means that my department does not have to sweat much. However,

7   whenever one of our customers forgets to pay, our computer "tickler" system, which Mensa

8   Gold, the chief administrative officer for the company, designed, prints out an alert sheet and

9   automatically sends a follow-up bill to the delinquent customer. Ninety-nine percent of the

10 time, payment immediately follows.

11

12 Even though I work for the company and am a twenty-five percent owner, I can take no credit

13 for the company's increase in value or in its wonderful reputation. My brother has been in

14 total control of production and sales. We have great relationships with our customers—in fact,

15 even with our suppliers. We're a small operation, but a stable, established one. That is why

16 people like to do business with us.

17

18 During our marriage, I lived and still live at 400 Schoolhouse Lane, Nita City, Nita. I was able

19 to buy the house because of my income, and the $1 million I received in YR-10 from a distri-

20 bution of assets generated by the sale of the company's manufacturing plants. The house is

21 5,500 square feet. There are five bedrooms, an office, a playroom, a family room, living room,

22 eatin kitchen, and a large finished basement. The home is on the shore in a very wealthy

23 community. I bought the home at a bargain price in July YR-8.

24

25 When we were first married, my marriage with Michael was almost perfect. Michael was

26 supportive and exciting. But things changed. When Loren was born on December 8, YR-10,

27 Michael devoted himself to her. He stopped working and became a "house dad." I agreed

28 with his decision. In fact, I used to say that I was the only feminist who had a wife. Things

29 were perfect. Unfortunately, Michael began to change. He stopped taking really good care of

30 Loren. I would come home after working and find her in a dirty diaper. It was obvious that the

1   diaper had been dirty for a long time because the stuff was all dry and sticking. She began

2   to get rashes that the doctor said were caused by irritation under the diaper. I knew that he

3   meant that the rashes were caused by not changing the diapers often enough. At about the

4   same time, Michael stopped taking care of the house, too. We had a cleaning person who

5   came twice a week to do the floors, bathrooms, the laundry, and change the sheets. But that

6   wasn't enough help for Michael. He couldn't find the time to pick up a toy, wash the dishes,

7   or even pick up the newspaper from wherever he happened to drop it. The breakfast dishes

8   would still be in the sink when I came home at 7:00 p.m. Toys were lying all over the floor in

9   every room. We had fights about his lack of care. I made it very clear that I felt that we had a

10   relationship. My job was working and making money to support us. His was caring for Loren

11   and the house. He said that I was a martinet. The lack of attention from Michael had an effect

12   on Loren. She had turned into a real brat. She was whiny and impossible because Michael

13   always let her do whatever she wanted. Some days she made you feel like strangling her. My

14   only refuge was leaving for work.

15

16   When I walked in one evening and tripped over a Grover doll that had been left in the entry,

17   I realized that I had to hire a live-in nanny to take care of Loren and the house. Linda Allen

18   was a find. She was young and loved Loren. I hired her in November YR-7. She seemed to get

19   along well with Michael. I didn't know how well for a long time.

20

21   I worked long hours during the week, but on the weekend the kids were mine. We had a

22   great time together. When Sasha was born, November 3, YR-6, the weekends were even

23   more fun. Being with me calmed Loren. By Sunday evening, I could control her a little. I had

24   full responsibility for her on the weekends. During the last three or four years, Michael would

25   just disappear. Since Linda was off, I had the kids all to myself. Each week, however, Michael

26   seemed to undue all of my efforts.

27

28   After I hired Linda, and after little Sasha was born, Michael started spending most of his day

29   away from the home. He left the child care completely up to Linda. The only thing he could

30   manage, despite the fact that he worked less than two full days a week, was to spend an

1   hour with the kids in between supper and their bedtime. He didn't even take Loren to her

2   after-school activities. Linda had to take her and truck Sasha along in the car. He began to

3   act just like the spoiled rich kid I first feared he might be. His family is quite rich. He went to

4   boarding school at Choate. His parents are separated, and his father has several houses, one

5   in Paris. He was raised by a team of nannies.

6

7   Starting in YR-5, Michael began to spend a lot of money. I don't understand exactly how. He just

8   started doing extravagant things. He had a professional chef come to the house to give him per-

9   sonal cooking lessons at $200 an hour. He bought a fully equipped gym and had a personal trainer

10   come to the house four days a week. By YR-4, his clothing bills exceeded $9,000 for the year.

11

12   I thought that they understood how I was killing myself to balance my desire to be with them

13   with my responsibility to bring in money to support the family. I only learned recently how

14   Michael has been poisoning Loren against me. I spent every weekend with Loren and Sasha

15   no matter how much I had to work. I came home every evening except when I had to travel,

16   and told them a story at bedtime. I went to all of Loren's school plays, even though it meant

17   taking time off from work. I was as involved as a working parent could be. But it seems that

18   Michael constantly told Loren that I was mean and that I didn't care for her or him. He has

19   really brainwashed the child.

20

21   We fought a lot during the last four years. Michael had started a small business but didn't

22   work at it. He is very talented and could easily make over $100,000 per year. He just doesn't

23   want to work. Even though he was making about $25,000 and I was making $200,000 plus my

24   stockholder's draw of $100,000, by YR-3 his expenditures were taking us over our budget. Our

25   sex life virtually disappeared. During YR-2, I don't think we had sex more than three times. It

26   became obvious to me that I was the worker ant and he was the grasshopper. I began to doubt

27   my values. It didn't make sense that I did all the work while he was loved by all and did nothing.

28

29   On December 15, YR-2, despite my increasing anger at his distance from me, I realized that

30   he was right. He was doing just what he wanted to with his life. I, on the other hand, was

1   slaving over collecting money from greedy companies. I had just had a miserable day. I had

2   spent the entire day with lawyers. When I got home, I told Michael that I couldn't stand it

3   anymore. I was going to quit. We would sell the big house and live on his income and my

4   distribution. He told me that I was crazy. He said he couldn't live like a pauper. I told him that

5   after ten years of living off me, he could go to work if he wanted. I said that we could live

6   on our combined—albeit lower—incomes. The next morning, Michael started a fight and

7   walked out on me.

8

9   I know that he started the fight on purpose. As I was in the hall bathroom on the second

10 floor checking my hair, I heard Michael talking to Linda in the hallway. They must have been

11 standing right outside of the bathroom. I heard Linda say, "If you are not too busy, how

12 about having lunch at The Homestead?" Michael then said, and I remember his exact words,

13 "I don't think that we will have time. I want you to get our stuff and the kids' things ready,

14 but make sure to watch the entryway when Friel comes to pick us Linda. I may need you."

15 I had no idea what that meant until later.

16

17 On the morning of December 16, Tommy came to pick me up. Tommy Friel picks me up

18 every morning and drives me to work. He works with me. He has been my best friend for

19 the past seven years. He lives a few miles from us. He stops by every morning and we drive

20 to work together. He also drives me home. We work long hours. I have occasionally had

21 to work through the night. Tommy would drive home alone on those nights. I was in the

22 foyer. I opened the door for Tommy. Then I went into the kitchen to get my pocketbook.

23 When I walked back into the foyer to leave, Michael seemed to appear out of nowhere

24 standing in front of the doorway to the kitchen, blocking my path to the front door. He

25 stood there and said the most vicious things. He accused me of having an affair with

26 Tommy. That is ridiculous, and Michael knows it. Tommy is gay and lives with his compan-

27 ion, Anthony Smith. Even though the kids were watching from the top of the stairs, he said

28 that I was a tramp and "screwing" Friel. Michael was vicious that morning. When I heard

29 him demeaning me and Tommy, I realized that this is what he had been planning when he

30 talked to Linda.

1   Michael was still blocking my path from the kitchen to the front door. When I tried to walk by

2   him, he moved to block my way with his body. He grabbed my arms so hard that they were

3   pinned to my sides. I tried to twist out of his grip. I couldn't do it. When he let go, I stumbled

4   backwards and would have fallen, but Tommy had come up behind us and caught me. Michael

5   said that I thrust him into the wall. That isn't true.

6

7   It is obvious that Michael was having an affair with Linda before he moved out. I saw them

8   holding hands on several occasions. Now I am worried about his affair influencing the chil-

9   dren. That is why I seek sole custody. On March 15, YR-1, I walked into his new house to pick

10   up the kids. Despite his insistence on having them, I still take care of them every weekend so

11   that he can "have some time to himself." Michael was lying with Linda on the couch. The kids

12   were sitting on the floor in front of them. The television was on. He had on boxer underpants.

13   She had on a robe. She was lying on top of him. As I started to enter the room, it looked like

14   they were having sex. The robe was open so that it lay on the couch on either side of Michael.

15   When I entered the room, she got up very quickly. She wasn't wearing anything under the

16   robe. It just isn't right. I couldn't stand the humiliation. I told Tommy about it, and he shocked

17   me by telling me all about Linda sleeping with Michael while she was working for me. I was so

18   upset that I looked through our old checking records. I know Michael. If he was having an affair

19   with Linda, he would have given her presents. That was when I found the check to Beautiful

20   Baubles for $1,500. I called the store and learned that he had bought a diamond and ruby

21   necklace. I remembered that I had seen Linda wearing one. Then, I knew for sure. I wasn't

22   suspicious before seeing the payment because I thought that her gaudy necklace was paste.

23   Couples separate every day. But nobody has an affair with the nanny in his wife's bed. He could

24   at least have gone to a hotel.

25

26   Until then, I had not realized how emotionally manipulative he is. I think that everyone should

27   know what he does with young vulnerable women like Linda. Everyone who we knew, I felt

28   that they should know that Michael could not be trusted.

1   As a result of this, at a function sponsored by the Hofstraconian Club on March 21, YR-1,

2   I talked to both Mrs. Victoria Windsor and Mr. Anson Able about Michael. When Mr. Able

3   asked me about the children's health, I told him that I was worried because Michael was

4   sharing his bedroom with their very much younger nanny. I also said that I was concerned

5   about the kids because Michael often acted as though he was trying to help them with their

6   emotional problems, as he had with our nanny, but was really seeking personal advantage in

7   our divorce.

STATEMENT OF LINDA ALLEN

1   I am twenty-four years old. I live with Michael Slovin and help take care of his two children,

2   Loren and Sasha. They are wonderful kids. I love them as though they were my own. I have

3   taken care of Loren since she was four years old and Sasha since he was born. I started work-

4   ing for the family in YR-7. I was almost eighteen and had just graduated from high school

5   when I saw an ad for an *au pair*. The ad said that they were looking for a "mother's helper,

6   with some housekeeping." I thought that would be a good way to get out of Sioux Falls, Idaho,

7   and applied for the job. They had placed ads in local papers in small cities throughout the

8   West. During the interview, I found out that I would actually be a "father's helper." I thought

9   that was neat and took the job. When I got to the Slovins's house, I found that there was a lot

10   more to do than I thought. Rita Slovin did nothing but work. She left Loren to be taken care of

11   by her husband, Michael. Her only involvement with the children was on the weekends. That

12   was Michael's "time off." It was the only time he had to take classes and relax from the twin

13   jobs of running the house and his business. Rita said horrible things about Loren. She would

14   call her "the monster" or "the brat." When she left to go to work, I once heard her say, "Thank

15   God, I can get out of here." Rita was never around. She hardly ever saw Loren, and later Sasha,

16   except when they went to bed and on the weekends. Except when she was out of town, she

17   only bothered to get home in time to put them to bed. I think that she may have read them a

18   brief story, but that was it. She left everything else to Michael.

19

20   Rita was very strict. Michael is a psychologist, and he was careful to let the children know that

21   they were trusted. He didn't want their diapers changed every second. He thought that would

22   undermine their self-confidence as they learned to control their bodies. He also felt that they

23   should be entitled to play anywhere in "their" house that they wanted. So he didn't insist that

24   toys and other things be removed before the children were finished playing. Rita cared more

25   for her personal convenience than she did about the development of the children. She went

26   into a fit if a diaper was wet or a toy was in the hallway or living room.

1   She verbally abused Michael. She always called him a "bum," even when they weren't

2   fighting. She had no respect for the effort he put into running a home and a business. She

3   would demean him by calling him her "wife." They argued often about his psychological

4   judgment about raising the children. Rita, who was never there, wanted the children to

5   be raised as though they were in a police state. Every toy picked up, every piece of stained

6   clothing made to disappear. They would shout. She often said that he just didn't want to

7   work. She didn't understand how much effort he put into his business. In YR-4, she once

8   yelled at him so loud that I could hear her while I was in Loren's room. One of the things she

9   screamed was that if he wanted to spend so much money on himself he could spend more

10   than two days a week working.

11

12   Despite everything that Rita did, Michael didn't let her unsettle the kids. He spent a lot of time

13   explaining Rita to the children. He tried to make them see how much she loved them despite

14   her absence and her abusing him. He would always tell them that she loved them, in her way.

15   He also told them that he understood how much she scared them but that she didn't mean to,

16   and that they would always have him, no matter what she did. I wish my father had held me

17   so close and cared for me as much.

18

19   Michael is a wonderful man, although he is far too occupied with his own work to do every-

20   thing alone. When I started working for them, he was starting a consulting business that

21   took almost all of his time. He had to be away from the house for most of the day and had

22   meetings in the evening as well. He was so caring for the kids despite his busy life. He made

23   sure to spend at least an hour with Loren, and later both of them, every day. He was very

24   involved with the kids. He monitored who they played with by carefully screening possible

25   playmates and giving me a list of those he approved. I was only allowed to make "playdates"

26   with children on his approved list. He also took the time to check into lessons and programs

27   that were appropriate for the kids. I was not allowed to enroll them in any program, from

28   Sasha's Gym for Tots to Loren's Modern Dance, unless it was on another list of programs

29   that he approved. He also made sure to know where I was taking them every day before he

30   left in the morning. I know that my father never spent any time with me. He was hardly ever

1   home except when he was drunk and abusive. Seeing a father as caring and involved with

2   his children changed my life.

3

4   Michael was very helpful to me. I left home a wreck. I was neglected by my parents. My

5   mother was always at work and my father was a drunk. I really raised myself. Michael seemed

6   to sense my need. He spent a lot of time with me from the first day I started working. He

7   would comfort me. He made me talk about my home life. He got me to work through my

8   developmental problems. I would often just hold him as I was talking about my childhood.

9   Over the years, I realized that I loved him. About two years after Sasha was born, Michael

10   let me see his needs. He opened up to me about how lonely it was to have a wife who didn't

11   understand him. I felt so important to be able to help him. He talked to me about every-

12   thing. I learned how Rita made him quit working because she couldn't stand being with

13   Loren and how her avoidance of the children had changed the way he felt for her. It was

14   clear that his love had disappeared as he saw how cold she was. All she cared about was her

15   family business and money.

16

17   Michael gave me presents to thank me for helping him with his problems, nice presents.

18   At first, he would give me a blouse or a dress from Bloomingdale's. By YR-3, he was giving

19   me wonderful presents. He gave me presents at Christmas, on my birthday, and Valentine's

20   Day. He gave me a gorgeous necklace, a pearl bracelet, diamond earrings, and other jewelry.

21   I know that the necklace cost over $1,000.

22

23   We never really had a physical relationship before he moved out. In YR-4, we kissed for the

24   first time. After that, I began to sleep in the same bed with him when Rita was on trips. We

25   never had sex—oral or otherwise. Michael said that it would be wrong. I really respected him

26   for that.

27

28   I know Anthony Smith. On January 3, I talked to Anthony about how much I liked my job and

29   how I felt sorry for my boss who was unhappy in his marriage. I also told him that I had got-

30   ten a very nice birthday gift from my boss and that I was sorry that I couldn't do anything in

1   exchange. I think he said that I could "give my boss some very personal services." I thought

2   that was a joke.

3

4   Tommy Friel drove Rita to and from work every day. He worked for her. He was quite nice. He

5   would talk to me sometimes when Rita wasn't ready to leave. I think that he had a "thing" for

6   Rita. He was supposed to be gay, but he put the moves on me. He once asked me if I wanted

7   to party with him. When I said no, he said that he thought I would enjoy doing a little cocaine

8   with him and his companion. I knew that he meant a date, though. He was always staring long-

9   ingly at Rita. Michael told me that they were having an affair. It was obvious.

10

11   On December 16, YR-2, Michael and I were going to have lunch at a very nice restaurant

12   called The Homestead. He had asked me to get my work out of the way early so that we

13   would have time for a nice lunch before the kids returned from school. When Friel came

14   to pick up Rita, Michael couldn't take it anymore. Michael saw them flirting and accused

15   them of having an affair. Friel couldn't deny it. He just hung his head and looked guilty. Rita

16   blew up. I was standing at the top of the stairs with Loren, but that didn't stop Rita. She

17   just screamed that Michael was a sorry excuse for a man and that she wanted him out of

18   her house. After she said she could "kill him," she ran into the kitchen, where there were

19   knives. When she returned, Michael tried to quiet her. He held her to calm her. She writhed

20   in his arms. She pushed Michael so hard that he smashed into the wall. I couldn't see him

21   because my view straight down was blocked, but I heard and felt the thump all the way up

22   on the walkway above the entry. Friel jumped in and grabbed Rita. Loren was confused.

23   She didn't understand what Michael was trying to do. She was crying and saying, "Daddy,

24   stop *hurting* Mommy." After that, Michael told them that he would leave but that he would

25   have to get a lawyer to see to it that the children were provided for. She said that she didn't

26   care. She meant that she didn't care about him or them. It was awful to hear a mother talk

27   like that.

28

29   I was standing at the top of the stairs because Michael told me that he wanted me to have

30   the kids out of their rooms and ready to leave as soon as Rita left. That is why we were up

1   there waiting. After Friel and Rita left, I packed the kids' and our stuff. Michael was still

2   hyper-excited by what Rita had done.

3

4   Michael's father had agreed to let Michael rent a house that he owned at a very reasonable

5   rent so that Michael could move in there. He set this up because he knew that he and Rita

6   were coming to an end. We moved in there with the kids. That night was the first time we

7   were intimate.

8

9   When we first started living together, I was very excited about it and the wonderful work that

10   Michael was doing. He got a great job and developed a big private practice. He was throttled

11   by Rita so that he was not able to spend the time on his practice. He could have done this

12   earlier, but he told me about how much consulting work he had to turn down because of Rita,

13   to limit how much business he had so that Rita wouldn't use his success as a reason to get out

14   of giving him his share of their joint money. Before moving out, he said, "It would cost me too

15   much money if I took these clients. I have to wait until I get my divorce." It was all because of

16   Rita and his concern that she would cheat him.

17

18   On March 21, YR-1, Michael and I attended a fundraising event for Everflash, his new

19   employer. I heard what Rita said about Michael to Mr. Anson Able, the chairman of the board

20   of directors of Everflash. I heard Rita's voice. She was standing behind me in a group that

21   included Anson Able and Victoria Windsor, dean of the Nita School, an elite private school

22   in Nita City. Rita was telling them awful lies about me and Michael. Rita said and this is an

23   exact quote, "Michael is a danger to any young woman, maybe even girl. He can't be trusted

24   if they are attractive. He will suck them into a relationship with him based on a claim that he

25   will help them with their emotional problems and then get them in bed."

STATEMENT OF TOMMY FRIEL

1   I am forty-five years old. I work for Rita Slovin as the assistant manager of the collection

2   division. She is the manager. She has done a wonderful job. She started right out of college.

3   I have a master's in business administration and was upset when she was put in a supe-

4   rior position. I soon learned, however, that she is a natural. The company is stable, but had

5   not grown in profitability in the decade since the founder died. The company's problems

6   were created when the founder died and Rita's brother George took over. He sold off our

7   manufacturing plants and switched to a system of having overseas contractors do all of our

8   manufacturing. This, unfortunately, raised our costs significantly. After he sold the plants, the

9   company's growth stopped because of a serious cash-flow problem that prevented the accu-

10   mulation of the capital necessary for expansion into foreign markets. George had really made

11   a major problem for the company because he not only sold the plants but he also made the

12   $4 million netted from the sale of the property available to the shareholders. I don't know

13   if he distributed it or, as someone in the legal department once told me, put it into lines of

14   credit that could be drawn upon in thirty-year, callable low-interest loans. All I know is that

15   the money was not available for corporate use. Without this money, the company had a

16   cash-flow problem. It was caused by delay in payments. We were averaging 18 months in col-

17   lection on accounts of over $100,000. There were very few deadbeats. Our regular accounts

18   had simply learned that they could take advantage of us. This meant that we had to finance

19   our cash-flow needs. It was a serious drain. When Rita took over, she solved the problem in

20   less than a year. I haven't been able to figure out exactly what she did. I finally decided it was

21   just the force of her personality that impacted on our customers. The result is that ninety-five

22   percent of our accounts pay within thirty days. We are an industry leader in this regard. Rita

23   has never recognized the importance of her accomplishment. She feels that she just made a

24   few calls and did nothing. She feels that she has been given a minor job because of her lack

25   of training and is overpaid. She is completely wrong.

26

27   I met Michael Slovin as soon as Rita started working for the company. I also immediately

28   realized that she was wrong to have married Michael. He really was a bum. He had her

1   wrapped around his little finger. As soon as he could, he stopped working. His excuse was to

2   take care of Loren. I know, however, that he seldom did much of the actual supervision of

3   Loren or Sasha. I have been stopping at Rita's home every morning and evening for almost

4   seven years. I pick her up and drop her off after work. It is convenient for both of us and

5   makes the drive fun. I have always liked Rita. But I have known that I am gay ever since I was

6   a boy. Rita and I do hug and hold hands from time to time, but that is because she is my good

7   friend. I would never cheat on Anthony. Before I finally admitted to myself that I would never

8   be happy unless I accepted my sexual identity, I tried to go out with women. Years ago, I did

9   have girlfriends. I was pretty successful at establishing friendships with women, but I never

10 felt comfortable with a sexual relationship with a woman.

11

12 Whenever I came into the house before Rita hired Linda Allen, it was a mess. Loren was always

13 dirty. Her face had food on it. She smelled from dirty diapers. The house was almost danger-

14 ously sloppy. Rita eventually gave up on Michael taking care of Loren and hired a nanny, Linda

15 Allen. But, Michael was Michael. A few years after they hired Linda, Michael started an affair

16 with her. I learned all about it from my companion, Anthony Smith. He has often met Linda

17 in the supermarket. They became friendly. She is really an innocent and decent person, but

18 Michael has conned her like he did Rita. She does all of the work, but thinks that he is wonder-

19 ful. He never deals with the kids, except for an hour or so in the evening. She does everything.

20 In January YR-3, Linda met Anthony in the store. She did not know that Anthony and I were

21 together. She never used any names, but she confided in him that her boss was "more than a

22 boss" and that "he was miserable in his marriage and was going to leave it as soon as he could

23 figure out how to do it right." She also told Anthony that her boss had given her the most

24 wonderful Christmas present. She said that her present to him had been "very personal ser-

25 vices." On March 1 or 2, YR-3, I was again shopping with Anthony. We dropped by the market

26 after work to get a few things for supper. Linda walked right by me and after some conversa-

27 tion with Anthony about the weather, he asked her about her boss. I heard Linda say, "He is

28 so exciting that it is hard to keep my hands off him until 'the wife' leaves in the mornings."

29 Anthony said something that I couldn't hear. I then heard her giggle, and she said, "And how!

30 When he left this morning I could hardly get out of bed." Anthony is an anthropologist. His

1   team got a large grant to fund a multi-year exploration in the northwest quadrant of the Gobi

2   Desert in Mongolia. He left three months ago and will not be back until June YR+1.

3

4   I didn't tell Rita about what Linda said because I thought that she would just get upset at

5   me. She knows that I have never liked Michael. I had often told her that he was a bad apple.

6   She was so deluded by Michael that I feared that she might just "kill the messenger." After

7   she told me about seeing Linda draped all over Michael with hardly a stitch on her, I told

8   Rita about the conversation I overheard between Linda and Anthony. She started to cry and

9   muttered something like, "I can't believe I ever let him touch me. I feel so dirty."

10

11   I was at their house on the morning of December 16, YR-2. I expected a scene because Rita

12   had told me that she was going to quit her job, sell the house, and go to law school. I told

13   her that Michael would never stand for that because all he wanted was her money. When

14   I arrived, I got more than I bargained for. Linda was at the top of the stairs with the kids.

15   Michael walked in and started accusing Rita of having an affair with me. Michael acted like

16   he was in a fury. Now that I think back, I believe that Michael was faking the whole fury thing

17   and that he was just trying to set Rita up. When Rita tried to leave, he stepped in front of her

18   and grabbed her. He held her arms against her sides and started to shake her. I thought that

19   he was going to hurt her. She was struggling to get away, but couldn't. I heard Loren shouting,

20   "Daddy is hurting Mommy," while he was shaking her. Seeing me approaching, he suddenly

21   let go and quickly stepped backwards. Rita's hands flew over her head as she tried to keep

22   from falling.

23

24   I am a member of the Hofstraconian Club. I was not at the event of March 21, YR-1. I heard

25   from several members that Rita told everyone about Michael's affair with Linda Allen. I was

26   told that she told everyone that Michael had been and was having an affair with the troubled

27   young woman who was their nanny.

STATEMENT OF LOREN SLOVIN

1   I was born on December 8, YR-10. I am in the fourth grade. My mother is Rita Slovin, and my

2   father is Michael. They argue a lot. In YR-2, Daddy, my brother, Linda, and I moved out of our

3   house. I miss it. Daddy said that we had to leave because Mommy didn't want us anymore.

4   I miss her, too, even though she wasn't with us very much. I loved the way she told us stories

5   and hugged us and took us places on the weekends. Daddy tells us that we owe everything to

6   her and always have to love her.

7

8   Daddy is my best friend. Before we moved, he and Linda did everything with us. He spent

9   time with us every day. When he wasn't there, Linda was. She is wonderful. She is our "other

10   mother." I like her a lot. She takes care of Daddy, too. He gives her presents to show her

11   that he wants her to be a member of the family, not just our nanny. He gave her a beautiful

12   necklace for Christmas YR-4. He said it was fake, but I heard Linda talking on the phone and

13   she said it was real diamonds and rubies. She let me wear it once.

14

15   Now that we all live together, Daddy and Linda hug and kiss more. Once they were on the

16   couch while we were watching TV. I don't think they saw me sneaking looks at them. Daddy

17   had his arms around Linda, and she was kissing him on the mouth. He was wearing his "house

18   shorts," and she had on a robe. She was lying on top of him. They did that for a long time. That

19   was when Mommy walked in. Mommy was coming to pick me and Sasha up so that we could

20   spend the weekend with her. She says that the door was open and she walked in because

21   nobody responded to the doorbell. The TV was on very loud. Mommy was mad.

22

23   Mommy is always mad and always tired now. I don't want to stay with her when she is that

24   way. Daddy is much nicer. Daddy is never too tired to read to me or Sasha. Now that we don't

25   live with Mommy, he isn't home as much. We spend several days every week at Mom's. He

26   used to make us breakfast and dinner a lot. Now, it is instant or Linda cooks. When I have

27   friends over, Daddy always does projects with us, just like in school. He even makes sure that

28   Sasha doesn't bug my friends and me when we are listening to our music downloads.

1   I want to live with Daddy and Linda. Sasha wants to, too. It's great having two grown-ups

2   around. Linda or Daddy are there a lot to play with me or to play with Sasha. Linda is always

3   there to help me with my homework and to make sure that Sasha does not annoy me.

4

5   Sasha can be a real pain and is always messing up my stuff. He has gotten even more hyper

6   since we moved. It's funny, but Sasha likes to be at our old house with Mommy. Whenever

7   we go back, Sasha giggles when we first go into our rooms and see our toys, and he always

8   tries to hog Mommy when she comes home from work. I get really annoyed at that. Daddy

9   says that Sasha is just younger and that I should try to be more patient. The other reason that

10   I really don't like to stay with Mommy is that she doesn't let me do what I want, like Daddy

11   does. When we stay at Mommy's house, she never lets me have "away" sleepovers. She says

12   that she hardly ever sees me, so she wants to spend as much time with Sasha and me as she

13   can. I was mad. Daddy always lets me have away sleepovers. I sleep over my friends' houses

14   a lot, now that I am in fourth grade. Last year, I told Daddy that Mommy said a huge "NO" to

15   sleepovers. Daddy says that it is selfish of Mommy.

16

17   There are a couple of good things about staying at Mommy's. One good thing is getting to

18   sleep in her big bed with her and Sasha. Mommy calls it camping out. She told me that she

19   hoped that camping out would make up for not having sleepovers. The other good thing is

20   that Mommy always makes sure that we have the latest stuff. I mean toys. She gets some of

21   it from work and from other places. She always says to us that she has connections. I had the

22   latest video games before anyone else. That's great. And another good thing is that Mommy

23   takes Sasha and me to work sometimes on Saturdays. She lets me try out the newest toys and

24   always asks me what I think. She tells me that I am a great help when it comes to toy testing.

25   Sasha tries toys out, but usually ends up breaking them. Mommy doesn't mind. She laughs

26   when I tell her that the toy isn't going to make it with kids like Sasha. I told Daddy. He thinks it

27   is great that Sasha and I help Mommy at work.

28

29   Mommy doesn't like Daddy. When we all lived together she used to yell at him and call him

30   bad names. I heard her call him a "bum." I don't know what she meant, but Daddy said it was

1   very mean of her. I think he is right because he was very upset. I sang him a song to make him

2   feel better. That was nice. It was a song that I sing to Mommy now when she is feeling mad

3   and tired.

4

5   Right before we left, Daddy and Mommy had a big fight in the hallway. Tommy had just come

6   to ride to work with Mommy. Daddy and Mommy shouted at each other. I was listening from

7   the balcony. Linda was with me. Mommy was standing in front of the door from the hallway

8   to the kitchen. Daddy walked towards Mommy and grabbed her. She tried to push him away.

9   Holding on to each other they almost fell down. I thought that they were going to knock

10   Tommy down. I yelled, "Stop, you're going to hit Tommy." But they didn't stop until Tommy

11   grabbed Mommy and pulled her away. Because of Tommy pushing Daddy, he fell and hit his

12   arm and the side of his face against the doorway. It made a big thud. I was scared for him. He

13   seemed all right. He got up, and he and Mommy kept talking. After Mommy left, Daddy said

14   that his arm really hurt. He went to the doctor later in the week. His arm was all swollen. It

15   turned yellow and blue and red. He showed me a bump on his forearm the size of an apple.

16   He said that was what Mommy had done when she pushed him.

17

18   Tommy is very nice. He gives me great presents. Daddy doesn't like him. He says that Tommy

19   is "doing Mommy." When I asked him what that meant, he said, "Nothing good."

20

21   The best thing is that both Mommy and Daddy live close to the GymNats Training Center

22   where I take my gymnastics classes. This year, I can go six days a week. I can't imagine not

23   training. I want to be the best. Sasha is a pill about it. He won't even go to see my competitions

24   when we are at Daddy's. Mommy, of course, makes him go.

Expert Report of Serena Phillips, MD
(Forensic Expert for Rita Slovin)

I am a psychiatrist who specializes in childhood and adolescent personality disorders. I am on the faculty of the Nita University Graduate School of Arts and Sciences and am part of the adjunct faculty of the Nita University School of Medicine. I lecture to both graduate and medical school students in my areas of specialization.

I received my BS and MS degrees in child and adolescent psychology from Harvard University in YR-15. I received my MD from Stanford University in YR-11. I did my internship and residency at Nita Memorial Hospital and completed my training in YR-7. I have been in private practice ever since that time.

I have a substantial private practice in Nita. All of my patients are children. The oldest patient is seventeen. In addition to my private practice, I donate time to public service activities. One of these is Best Interests of Children's Health. It is a group of mental health professionals who offer their services to children in need of mental guidance but whose parents do not have adequate medical insurance coverage and cannot afford to pay for us. I met Rita Slovin through my involvement with Children's Health. Her company, Perfect Toys, donates toys and child-size furniture to our organization. When I was speaking to Rita Slovin concerning a shipment of Perfect Toys' latest donation, she mentioned that she was going through a divorce and asked if I did consulting work in custody matters. I told her that I did not, but was interested in working in the field. Rita Slovin then asked me if it would be appropriate for her attorney to call me. I said that I would not mind. I do not need the income. I earn approximately $350,000 a year from my practice. I thought it would be interesting to explore the forensic psychiatry field. Her attorney called me the next day. I was retained by her attorney. This is the first time that I have been asked to evaluate the emotional health of children as part of a legal custody battle in the context of a divorce situation. I have not yet submitted a bill for my services but I plan to do so, shortly. I understand that the "going rate" is $250 hour for preparatory work and $5,000 per day for deposition or trial testimony.

I have been asked to render an expert opinion on the appropriate custodial status for the two children of Rita and Michael Slovin. I have been informed by both Mr. and Mrs. Slovin and by Mrs. Slovin's attorney that the parents are in conflict over the custody of the two children. Each wants sole custody of both children. Despite that conflict, both parents unequivocally agree that the two children should not be split and should remain together, no matter what the final custody outcome. I agree with that conclusion and have accepted it as a premise for my examination.

I met both the Slovin children separately and together, and I have observed them with their parents. In all, I have spent approximately ten hours of observation time and have had at least five hours alone with Loren Slovin (age ten), the elder of the two children. I have met with Sasha Slovin (age six) alone for approximately one hour. I have also had extensive conversations with Michael and Rita Slovin.

The parents are in dispute with regard to several interrelated issues. The predominant issue is custody. Each parent wants sole custody of the two children. What that means is that each parent wants the children to reside with him or her and for that parent to have sole authority with regard to any decisions regarding the children. The nonresidential parent would be given visitation rights and would be notified with regard to major decisions concerning the children. The children currently reside with the father and visit with the mother.

Conclusion

Based on the factors that I will detail below, it is my recommendation that Rita Slovin should be awarded sole custody of the children, with exclusive right of decision making. Michael Slovin, however, should receive liberal visitation rights. It is in the best interests of those children that they remain in the house in which they have been raised and where they would be most comfortable and which would give them the most stability. It is readily apparent from my extensive sessions with the children that Rita Slovin will provide them with a much healthier and stable, loving, family-oriented environment.

Michael Slovin—the nature of the relationship between Michael Slovin and the children, and the impact of his relationship with Linda Allen:

My clinical evaluation of the children revealed that Michael Slovin has systematically developed inappropriate relationships with both children.

1) Improper Influence. He has improperly influenced both Loren and Sasha and has displayed flawed decision making in placing his children in inappropriately awkward situations.

A) Sasha. It became obvious that Michael was using this inappropriate relationship to impair the relationship between Sasha and his mother. Sasha said that his father was often sad because "Mommy wants to work more than she wants to be with us." He also said that "We don't know how much Mommy loves us because she is a workaholic." He could not explain what a "workaholic" was.

When Sasha was asked what he wanted to be when he grew up, he responded that he wanted to be "like his father" because "I want to have two wives. A man needs two women. One to be kind and take care of him when he is sad, and the other to be smart and earn money." When he was asked what two women Daddy had, he said, "Linda to hug and kiss him when he is sad and Mommy to earn money for us." It is obvious that a five-year-old would not verbalize such a response on his own. It is indicative of the fact that Michael Slovin has developed an inappropriately mature relationship with Sasha, in which Michael shares his personal feels and the intimate nature of his relationships.

He currently presents symptoms of depression, the onset of which occurred after the father relocated the children to an apartment with Linda Allen. Sasha says that "I love both Linda and Mommy." He said that he first realized how important Linda was to Daddy when he saw them kissing in the kitchen the day after her birthday. He described the kiss as "weird." His attention deficit disorder is certainly aggravated by the tension of the separation.

B) Loren. Michael seems to have developed the same type of inappropriately adult relationship with Loren. My sessions with Loren indicate that although she is fond of Linda Allen, she perceives her father's relationship with her as improper. Loren has explained that her father has had many talks with her about Linda Allen. He apparently has asked Loren's opinion as to whether he and Linda Allen should get married. According to Loren, her father told her that he did not want to, that marriage is old fashioned, and that the formality of marriage means nothing if two people truly love each other. Michael Slovin's act of employing his ten-year-old daughter as confidante is entirely inappropriate. As a parent, and especially as a PhD social worker, Michael Slovin should separate his personal, intimate feelings from his young children in order to provide them with the proper nurturing environment. While it is arguably appropriate to consult one's young child over a food or clothing choice, one should not pressure a young child to help one decide intimate, life-altering issues. Loren relayed that conversation to me in a session and indicated that she was upset that her father would talk to her in that way and that she did not feel good after the talks. When she told her father that she did not like him to talk to her about those things, Michael Slovin apparently told her that she should experience all kinds of feelings and that her discomfort was a kind of feeling that is good for her to recognize. Michael Slovin's selfish behavior in that regard is damaging to a child like Loren, who is having difficulty with her parents' divorce.

Loren expressed concern over the relationship between her father and Linda Allen. She indicated that she felt a little uncomfortable with "Linda" now that her parents were getting divorced. She explained that although she thought it was "OK that Daddy found someone else," she was worried that things would not be the same once they moved, that it would be "Daddy's and Linda's house," and that they were not a true family. She confided to me that she had talked with Michael Slovin about her "feelings." She told me that Michael Slovin told her that she had to get used to dealing with "grown-up" feelings and what she was experiencing was good for her. She also told me that Michael Slovin ended the conversation by reminding Loren how much "Mommy worked," and how "Mommy never has any time. That is why we are lucky to have Linda."

Those remarks by Michael Slovin demonstrate his inability to segregate his personal feelings and hostilities from the emotional needs of his child. Finally, it should be noted that during the session where Loren revealed those concerns, Michael Slovin unexpectedly appeared in the office. Once he was in the room, Loren suddenly volunteered, "I like Linda and consider Linda my 'other mother.'"

C) Linda Allen. It has been my experience as a child therapist that a parent's extramarital relationship can be confusing to that parent's children. Young children do not understand the complexities of adult relationships. They see the world in black and white terms. Adults who live together should be married. If they live together and are not married, or if they are living in a marital situation and are having an affair with another person, the children see that something is wrong. It is therefore the parent's obligation to shield the children from such a difficult situation. Michael Slovin has done the opposite. From the comments of the children, it appears that he permitted them to see an inappropriately intimate relationship between himself and Linda Allen prior to the time of his separation from Rita Slovin. The fact that these acts occurred in the marital residence, in front of the children, are glaring examples of his lack of self-control. In light of his professional training in the field, it is almost contemptuous of the emotional turmoil that predictably would be induced in the children. Further emotional trauma is certain if he continues to engage in intimate activities in front of the children. Although it is a fact that separated parents will develop new relationships, a predominant concern must be in protecting the children from excessive exposure to inappropriate sexuality. For Linda Allen to be lying on top of Michael Slovin, dressed only in a robe that was completely open and while he was barely dressed, is dramatic proof of his unsuitability to maintain the role of custodial parent. Rather than gradually let the children adjust to his new relationship, he plunged them into an entirely alien atmosphere. Linda Allen is not a stranger to them. However, the children knew her solely as an employee, a "nanny." Then Michael Slovin treated her as a "wife," and now he has told them to treat Linda Allen as the children's mother.

That attitude can only serve to damage the children emotionally and serves no purpose other than to feed Michael Slovin's self-interest.

2) Undermining Maternal Relationship. Michael Slovin appears to have exploited his inappropriate relationship with both children to undermine their relationships with Rita Slovin. He consistently belittles her in front of them. Loren has confided in me that Michael Slovin has told Sasha and her that Rita Slovin is more concerned with her job than her children and that if the children were to live with Rita Slovin, she would never be home. She would hire a staff of people to take care of them. He has also engaged in verbally abusive behavior directed against Rita Slovin in front of the children. According to Loren, he has called her "pig," "jerk," and other such epithets during telephone conversations he has had with Rita Slovin, which conversations Loren and Sasha overheard. Loren related one incident that occurred when Michael Slovin had come to the former family home to pick up the children. It was in the afternoon. Rita Slovin had taken the day off to be with the children. Michael Slovin, upon entering the home, yelled, "So, slut, having your boyfriend run things for a change?" Loren confided that Rita Slovin was so upset that she ran into the den, in tears. When Loren asked Michael Slovin what a "slut" meant, he told her that he said, "Slovin," and not "slut." Loren intimated that she did not believe her father. Those incidents demonstrate Michael Slovin's inability to monitor his behavior and are indicative of a narcissistic pattern of self-absorption.

3) Best Interests of the Children. During my talks with Loren, while she has expressed a desire to live with her father, she confided how much she loves and feels sorry for her mother. She has specifically said that "Daddy has Linda. Mommy has no one. Without me, Mommy would be all alone. That is so very sad." According to Loren, her favorite activity is playing with "Mommy" or her friends. It is obvious she liked to play with "Mommy" best because she often did not see her during the week. Loren told me that her mother worked hard during the week and often came home too late to do anything but read them a story and kiss them goodnight. I learned from Loren that her mother not only came home late, but left the house many mornings before the children were awake. Sasha also prefers to stay with his father: "Daddy is fun. He is my best buddy."

However, a more extensive exploration of the nature of the allocation of the child rearing activities between Michael and Rita Slovin revealed the extent to which Michael's manipulative conduct had effected the children's perceptions. Although the children repeat Michael Slovin's statements about Rita Slovin, she has, in fact, been the primary caretaker and caregiver. Michael Slovin admitted his weaknesses in these areas. He has conceded that he is not the neatest person, and despite his degrees in psychology, he has more of a *laissez-faire* attitude with the children.

Although Michael left his employment when Loren was born, he did not actually care for the children. His inability to accept the restrictions of a homemaker's life forced Rita to hire a fulltime, live-in nanny (Linda Allen). Rita Slovin was so upset over Michael Slovin's lassitude that she had been curtailing her work day to come home to take over his responsibilities on many occasions, especially before Linda Allen was hired. Once Linda Allen was hired, Michael's interaction with the children appears to have been more restricted than Rita's. However, Michael's absences were caused by personal choices (he spent a large amount of time in recreational and cultural pursuits such as physical fitness, language and cooking classes, etc.). Rita was absent because of her employment. On the typical day, both parents agree that Michael set the schedule for the children. That schedule was then implemented by Linda Allen. Michael returned to have dinner with the kids. On the weekends, Linda Allen was not working and Rita assumed full responsibility for the children. She did everything with them. Michael agreed with this assessment. He said, "The weekend was my free time." Since the week was free, too, because of Linda Allen, my conclusion is that he has created the impression of being the primary parent without having actually done the work. Further evidence of this developed when I asked about doctors' appointments and the like. I discovered that Rita arranged for the children's activities and made sure that the doctors' appointments were kept, and that the children were properly fed and maintained proper personal hygiene. Indeed, Michael said that "Rita has a secretary. Why shouldn't she take care of that stuff."

Conclusion

In sum, it is my recommendation that Rita Slovin be granted full custody of her children. Michael Slovin should be granted full visitation. A custodial plan awarding Michael Slovin joint decision-making authority with Rita Slovin is not viable given Michael Slovin's history of poor judgment. Although Rita Slovin was unable, until now, to provide the daily care giving to her children, she has been the sole primary caretaker of those children in terms of their global emotional needs and the protection of their interests. She, apparently, was the sole parent to provide structure for the children.

Attachment A
Extract of Treatise on Attention Deficit Disorder

Jones, Smith, & Hopkins, *Emotional Traumas of the Young* (Harper & James, YR-1), page 78:

"One of the clearest certainties in the very uncertain world of causative factors concerning the development of attention deficit disorder [ADD] is the role of stress. Especially vulnerable to this process is the young male. Presently unknown factors in the biology of the male development seem to predispose boys to a process in which situational stress contributes to the alteration of the chemical balance in the body and the concomitant development of ADD symptomology. Stress management therapy is, thus, an important part of the developing treatment strategies."

CURRICULUM VITAE

Serena Phillips, MD
9 Mockingbird Lane
Port Nita, Nita 09998

Date of Birth:	8/15/YR-55
Place of Birth:	Darien, Connecticut
Spouse:	Steven Eckhardt, PhD
Children:	Forrest Phillips-Eckhardt
	Giovanna Phillips-Eckhardt

Academic Background

BS, Harvard University, Cambridge, Massachusetts	YR-25
MS, Harvard University, Cambridge, Massachusetts	YR-23
MD, Stanford University, Berkeley, California	YR-19
Internship Program in Adolescent Medicine Nita Memorial Hospital, Nita City, Nita	YR-19 to YR-18
Residency in General Psychiatry Nita Memorial Hospital, Nita City, Nita	YR-18 to YR-16
Residency in Child Psychiatry Nita Memorial Hospital, Nita City, Nita	YR-16 to YR-14
Fellowship in Adolescent Psychiatry Children's Hospital, Nita City, Nita	YR-14 to YR-12

Professional Background

YR-12 to present	Child and Adolescent Psychiatrist, Private Practice 608 Meritor Boulevard, Nita City, Nita

Appointments

YR-11 to YR-9	*Lecturer, Adolescent Mood Disorders* Nita Memorial Hospital

YR-11 to YR-9	*Adjunct Professor, Child and Adolescent Psychiatry* Nita University School of Medicine
YR-10 to YR-5	*Volunteer Adolescent Psychiatric Consultant* Worldwide Children's Volunteer Services
YR-5 to present	*Director of Mental Health Professionals* Best Interests of the Child's Health

Publications

Marino, Phillips, Wechsler, "Adolescent Bipolar Disorders," Conference on Adolescent Psychiatric Disorders, Orlando, Florida YR-12

Phillips, Sullivan, "Poster: Developing Patterns of Deviant Behavior," Conference on Adolescent Psychiatric Disorders, Orlando, Florida YR-10

Phillips, "Suicidal Ideations in the Female Adolescent," *Journal of the American Academy of Child and Adolescent Psychiatry*, June YR-8

Honors

YR-18	Bascomb Award for Achievement, Nita Memorial Hospital Internship Program
YR-16	Bascomb Award for Achievement, Nita Memorial Hospital Residency Program
YR-14	Lorna Davis Memorial Prize in Child and Adolescent Psychiatry, Nita Memorial Fellowship Program
YR-10	Mental Health Professional of the Year, Volunteer Doctors of Nita

Expert Report of Soren Elkind, PhD
(Forensic Expert for Michael Slovin)

I am a child psychologist. I received my BS in psychology from Nita University in YR-20, and my MS in YR-15 and PhD in YR-10, both from Gorganza University here in Nita. I did begin my graduate studies immediately after receiving my undergraduate degree. I worked as a clinical social worker for the Nita State Department of Youth upon graduation and remained there through completion of my master's degree. I then began my own practice as a psychologist, specializing in child and adolescent behaviors. My doctoral dissertation was entitled *Divorce in the Nursery: A Study of the Effects of Parental Discord on Infants*. The findings reported in my dissertation were based on clinical studies I performed in the context of my practice.

In YR-4, I was appointed chair of the Child and Adolescent Psychology Program at the Gorganza Institute, which is a privately funded hospital and is part of Gorganza University. My responsibilities are both administrative and clinical. I supervise graduate psychology students with their patient loads, conduct a weekly seminar called "On the Vanguard of Child Psychology," oversee scheduling and personnel matters, and act as a liaison between the Institute and the University. Because of my experience and my position at the Institute, I am often hired as a forensic psychologist in custody litigations. I testify, at trial or deposition, in over ten cases each year. Although both mothers and fathers have hired me, because of my reputation for fairness and commitment to family I have never been involved in a case in which I have had the opportunity to be called as a witness by the mother in a custody litigation. Last year alone, I earned $250,000 as a forensic psychologist. My salary as chair is $90,000.

Michael Slovin's attorney and I have worked on other cases in the past. In fact, she recommended me to Michael Slovin, who retained me on the spot. I have met with Michael Slovin and his partner, Linda Allen, and with Loren and Sasha Slovin. It is my recommendation that Michael Slovin be given full physical custody of Loren and Sasha and that Mr. and Mrs. Slovin should share joint decision-making authority regarding both children. Thus far, I have been paid $25,000 for my services in this matter. I send bills to Michael Slovin's attorney, who pays me directly.

My conclusion is based on the extensive sessions I have had with the above-named people. I have also read Dr. Serena Phillips's report. While I have long admired Dr. Phillips professionally, I take issue with her methods and conclusions. With regard to her methods, she did not conduct any quality time sessions with the younger of the two Slovin children, Sasha. She also apparently did not spend any time with Linda Allen. She therefore could not possibly have conducted a thorough forensic evaluation of the family situation. I also feel that she has taken an adversarial role in this case rather than maintaining her usual standards of professionalism. In particular, I am disturbed by the fact that she has abandoned her long-stated views on the importance of the caretaker in the decision-making role of child development. To demonstrate this unprofessional conduct, I have attached a short excerpt from the testimony she gave in a custody case and a quote from her paper—Phillips, Sullivan, "Poster: Developing Patterns of Deviant Behavior," from the Conference on Adolescent Psychiatric Disorders, Orlando, Florida, YR-10—to my report.

I recommend that Michael Slovin be awarded sole physical custody of the children. The reason is simple. Michael Slovin has, for all intents and purposes, had sole physical custody of the children even prior to the divorce litigation. My sessions with all concerned revealed that Michael Slovin has been the true caregiver to the children ever since they were born. Michael Slovin gave up his career as a clinical social worker to raise Loren and Sasha. The children, especially Loren, are most cognizant of his importance as a stay-at-home father. Loren has mentioned that she did not like the fact that her father was planning to return to work. She wanted him to stay home and be with her brother and her. When I asked her about Linda Allen, Loren remarked that she liked Linda Allen and wanted her to be at home, too.

Loren is an active, intelligent ten-year-old. She participates in social and physical activities in and outside of school. She is an extremely talented gymnast. She has a mature degree of selfawareness concerning the stresses occasioned by the divorce of her parents.

Sasha is a very active six-year-old. He shows no superficial signs of stress caused by the parents' separation. He does exhibit some symptoms of hyperactivity. However, hyperactivity is a physical disease and is not the product of situational pressures. Extensive discussions, however, produce classic signs of avoidance and distress. He fears the loss of his father and has focused most of his security needs on the person of his father. When talking about his time with his father, he is particularly animated and almost gleeful. The contrast to the serious demeanor when discussing his mother is striking.

The reason for Sasha's attachment to his father is clear. Michael Slovin's life, especially prior to the arrival of Linda Allen in the house, was devoted to the children. Linda Allen has helped him with his caretaking responsibilities, but she has not alleviated him of them. Michael Slovin, as Rita Slovin has conceded, was in charge during the day. In tandem with Linda Allen, who had been employed to do much of the day-to-day care as the parties' nanny prior to the litigation, Michael Slovin was the primary caregiver. He instructed Linda Allen as to what to feed the children and what activities they should be involved in. According to Linda Allen, while they all resided in one house, she took care of the details, while Michael Slovin was the parent in charge. Rita Slovin was rarely home during the week, and when she was, according to Linda Allen, she spent most of her time in her home office, working. Her only contact with the children was on the weekends. During the week, she just read them bedtime stories and occasionally had dinner with them.

Both Loren and Sasha agree that Michael Slovin was and remains the primary caretaker. When asked, "Who takes you to school?" the children simultaneously answered, "Daddy or Linda." When asked, "Does Mommy ever take you to school?" Loren answered, "She's too busy. She is too important. But Daddy says that we have to forgive her. She makes our money." Sasha did not respond to the question. The children also responded that Michael Slovin or Linda Allen made their breakfast, prepared their lunches, and made them dinner. In short, Michael Slovin was the consistent presence, along recently with Linda Allen, in the children's lives. Rita Slovin has conceded that prior to the divorce action, she had devoted much of her time to her family business. She mentioned that she had a "large monthly nut" to pay and that Michael Slovin did not contribute to the family income at all. Therefore, the financial burdens fell on her shoulders, according to Rita Slovin. She did indicate that she planned to resign her position at her family business and devote more time to the children. As of the date of this report, she has not yet done so.

I contacted Rita Slovin to schedule a session with her. She had to cancel the session due to illness; she never called to reschedule the appointment. At the time she canceled, I spoke with her at length over the telephone and essentially obtained the information I needed to complete my report. In my telephone conversation with Rita Slovin (which was approximately thirty minutes in length), she acknowledged the importance of Michael Slovin in the children's lives. She remarked that he supervised the "nitty-gritty" of the children's lives and was "down in the trenches." She added that she admired Michael Slovin for dealing with all those "brainless mothers" who did nothing but "hang out at the gym and at Starbucks." She explained that her children's popularity with other children was due to "Linda's" (which I assumed meant Michael and Linda since he supervised all her activities) help in arranging play dates, sleepovers, etc. Rita Slovin admitted that she did not like doing such things and would find it "tiring" to drive the children around all day.

Rita Slovin has, however, spent time with the children on the weekends. Michael Slovin has consistently enabled Rita Slovin to spend this time with the children by yielding to her on the weekends. During these few days, she explained that she enjoyed her children's company and wanted to spend as much time as she could with them. Rita Slovin's candor reveals her weaknesses regarding parenting. To increase her time with the children, she denied them play dates and sleepovers on the weekend. This isolation from the peer group experience stifles the children's emotional growth and may hamper their ability to interact as adults. Rita Slovin's disinterest in her children's social experiences is not healthy. She has not taken her children's best interests into consideration, but rather has played into her own neuroses and self-interest by tying them to her.

I believe that the presence of Linda Allen in the household with Michael Slovin and the children is a strong, positive factor mitigating toward granting him custody. Michael Slovin has chosen a new life partner. The children are very familiar with Linda Allen, who has acted as a co-primary caretaker for the children for many years. Her transition from employee to their father's partner should not seem strange to Loren and Sasha. The two children recognize her importance by responding to questions about her with: "We like Linda. Daddy is lucky to find her. He says that all the time. We are lucky, too." In my sessions with Linda Allen, she displayed a sensitivity to the children's needs that I have found rare in a person in her particular situation. She explained that she has not tried to usurp Rita Slovin's status as mother, but realized that the children needed a daily maternal caretaker. That was a role that Rita Slovin was reluctant to undertake, but one that Linda Allen gladly assumed. Linda Allen was quite candid about her relationship with Michael Slovin. She easily admitted that Michael Slovin had let her become the "detail person," that he was also not the neatest person in the world, and how shocked she was over the lack of cleanliness regarding the house and the children. She, however, did not fault Michael Slovin for those shortcomings. "He gives so much of himself to the children," she said. "You have to admire him for his devotion." She said that once she arrived, Michael Slovin was not anxious to relinquish his responsibilities, even in part, to Linda Allen. Gradually, however, she has been able to ease him of the ministerial burdens, permitting him to take classes, go to the gym, and work on reasserting himself in his professional community. She now is allowed to take the children to all of their "play date appointments," prepare and give them their meals, and transport them to classes and friend's houses. The only time that she is excluded from these activities is on the weekends. Rita Slovin dominated the children and insisted on doing everything with them on those days.

Although Michael Slovin and Linda Allen at the time of this report do not intend to get married, that is not an important factor in this custody recommendation. The concept of the nuclear family has changed dramatically over the past fifteen years. Marriage is not dispositive of family stability. What is dispositive is the strength of the relationship of the parental figures. Michael Slovin and Linda Allen have sufficiently demonstrated to me their long-term commitment to each other and to the children. They have confided in me that they see their relationship as a permanent one and acknowledge that they would have to work hard to make the children feel comfortable with the relationship. They have had candid talks with the children about their relationship and the transition and adjustment all would have to make. Linda Allen and Michael Slovin agreed in their assessment that the children understood the new situation and that they were excited about their new home. The claims of inappropriate sexuality made by Rita Slovin are typical of the separated spouse who has difficulty adjusting to the new single life. She is simply seeing impropriety in the type of intimacy that should be the hallmark of a family. In particular, the fact that Linda Allen and Michael Slovin were acting, according to Rita Slovin, "improperly," merely because they were "cuddling" on a couch while the children watched television, is indicative of the warmth of their relationship and the trust that they and the children share. I detected no concerns about this or any intimate conduct between Michael Slovin and Linda Allen in my discussion with the children. If the warmth of their relationship has any significance on the issue of custody, it is to favor leaving the children with Michael Slovin.

It is clear from the above that Michael Slovin, as current primary caretaker, should continue in that role and be granted sole physical custody. Rita Slovin does appear to love her children; however, I do not believe that she is emotionally equipped to take on the day-to-day caretaking that would be required of her. She has not been willing to do so in the past. It is clear that she is not willing to do so now. She has not resigned from her company. She refuses to make any effort to have her children interact with their peers. Those crucial points demonstrate Rita Slovin's unfitness as a sole custodial parent. In drawing that conclusion, I have discounted remarks from Linda Allen regarding Rita Slovin's temper and her habit of harshly admonishing the children and speaking abusively to Michael Slovin.

Attachment A

1) Excerpt from testimony of Dr. Serena Phillips, who was called as an expert by a mother who was challenging her ex-husband's motion for sole physical custody with exclusive right of decision making (*In the Matter of Sally K.*, January 27, YR-3, Nita County Court, Nita):

* * *

Q: Dr. Phillips, I pose the following hypothetical to you. Suppose that a couple are separated and are planning to divorce. The mother has been the primary caretaker for the couple's three children. The father seeks not only sole custody on the ground that the mother had a substance abuse problem but on other factors as well. The mother has undergone rehabilitation and is doing well. The children indicate that they love their mother. The father also recognized that the mother has been the primary caretaker. Do you understand those hypothetical facts?

A: Yes, I do. However, I do need to know the following. How old are the children?

Q: The children are twelve, eight, and six years of age, and are all girls.

Q: Based on those hypothetical facts, would it be proper to grant the father sole custodial rights?

A: No, it would not be right. The mother has been the primary caretaker for her three daughters. Her relationship with her children and the stability and benefits it has created for the children, by virtue of that responsibility, should not be destroyed. The fact that the mother exercised poor personal judgment with her substance abuse should not predominate in determining such a life-altering issue for the children. The role of the primary caretaker is the most important role in the development of children. Unless the mother is actively unfit through demonstrated patterns of abuse, the mother, who has been the primary caregiver through the first five or more years of a child's life, should always be part of the decision-making process concerning that child.

2) Excerpt from Phillips, Sullivan, "Poster: Developing Patterns of Deviant Behavior," Conference on Adolescent Psychiatric Disorders, Orlando, Florida, YR-10, page 126:

"The relationship between a child and the maternal caregiver during the child's formative pre-school years is the dominant relationship in the child's development. The modern legal trend towards severing the child from the decision-making patterns associated with this caregiver is one of the many factors that have produced an explosion of adolescent deviance."

CURRICULUM VITAE

Soren Elkind, PhD
12 Washburn Court
Nita Point, Nita 09988

Academic Background

BS, Social Work	Nita University, Nita City, Nita	YR-20
MS, Psychology	Nita University, Nita City, Nita	YR-15
PhD, Psychology	Gorganza University, Nita City, Nita	YR-10

Professional Background

YR-20 to YR-15	Clinical Social Worker, Nita State Department of Youth, Nita City, Nita
YR-15 to YR-4	Child Psychologist, Private Practice, 75 North End Avenue, Nita City, Nita
YR-6 to present	Professor, Child and Adolescent Psychology Program, Gorganza Institute, Nita City, Nita
YR-4 to present	Chair, Child and Adolescent Psychology Program, Gorganza Institute, Nita City, Nita
YR-4 to present	Forensic Consultant, Private Practice, 75 North End Avenue, Nita City, Nita

Publications

Doctoral dissertation: *Divorce in the Nursery: A Study of the Effects of Parental Discord on Infants*, YR-10, Gorganza University, Nita City, Nita

Elkind, *Adolescent Psyche in a Nutshell* (Jaguar Publications, YR-5)

Elkind, *Parental Impact on a Child's Choice in Divorce: A Guide for Lawyers and Laypeople* (Gorganza University Press, YR-3)

Elkind, *Understanding the American Child: A Text for the Modern Psychology Student* (Gorganza University Press, YR-2)

Honors

YR-5   Florida Award for Excellence in Teaching, Gorganza Institute, Nita City, Nita

MODULE 2

NEGOTIATING THE CHILD CUSTODY CASE

BACKGROUND INFORMATION FOR NEGOTIATIONS: INSTRUCTIONS

1) For the purpose of all negotiation exercises, you are to assume that you have had prior contact with the attorney representing the other party.

2) All negotiators proceed under the assumption that all parties want to settle the matter. This does not mean that the client's desires or her interests can be ignored to reach a settlement. It does mean, however, that a substantial effort should be made to find mutually satisfactory resolutions to the disputed issues, and to convince the other party to accept them or reasonable alternatives.

3) Before each negotiation, you must have a negotiation plan, which must include:

   a) the starting position and the reason for this position;

   b) any concessions or accommodations that are planned;

   c) the interests or rights that are perceived to be those most critical to gaining an agreement;

   d) the settlement goal or the designed point of agreement;

   e) the "final" position if you have a final position, and the alternative for your client if you cannot achieve this result.

Brief Overview of Negotiation Planning

Structure of Negotiation Preparation

Negotiation preparation requires you to have gone through, at least, the following planning steps, as discussed below:

- negotiation planning and basic strategy;

- implementation of the negotiation plan.

Negotiation Planning and Basic Strategy

Preparation starts with analyzing the "rights-based" strengths and weaknesses of your client's position. You must carefully analyze each of the rights-based issues. Be sure to assess the specific facts of the case when making this analysis.

Continue your preparation continues by identifying the "interest-based" issues and evaluate each such issue. Begin this evaluation by assessing the degree to which each "interest" is shared by the parties and the strength of the commitment of each to that value.

Then move to "strategic gaming."[2] Although the analytic process is similar, the preparatory "gaming" process is simpler in a purely rights-based situation. Gaming in a predominantly *rights-based negotiation*, such as in the equitable distribution problem, means assessing how much each side is likely to modify its economic demands (or offers) to reflect its chances of success at trial—and the value of avoiding the risk of loss at trial.

Gaming in an *interest-based negotiation*, such as in the custody negotiation, requires more complex planning. First, you must identify the differing positions of each party. Second, you must analyze the disputed issues to arrive at potential mutually agreeable accommodations. This is a critical step in planning. While it is true that solutions may develop during the negotiation process and no negotiator should be so wedded to prior planning that an unexpected alternative is dismissed, the best negotiation technique involves identifying a series of potential resolutions prior to negotiation. In thinking about accommodations, you should consider:

- conforming to the client's authorization, which requires substantial counseling (almost negotiating at times) with the client to gain authority for compromises;

- meeting the interests of the other party;

- developing both compromises[3] and/or exchanges.[4]

---

2. Gaming is used to refer to the process of creating, justifying and supporting specific demands that are primarily presented for the purpose of reaching a pre-determined but different result. The "game" of the negotiator is akin to the process of bargaining at a flea market or in the bazaar. Everyone knows that the item will be sold for less than is asked and more than is offered. But, the exact price will only be determined by the skill with which the parties participate in the "game."

3. *Compromises* are changes in position towards a common middle.

4. *Exchanges* are concessions on one or more issues that are made for equal concessions by the other party on other issues.

Third, you must visualize the accommodations (including compromises and/or exchanges) that the other party might propose to the negotiation. In this process, you must construct the potential justifications the other party will use to support the reasonableness of its accommodations.

Warning: Do not let the joy of "game playing" destroy the chances of reaching an agreement. In interest-based negotiations, clients almost always want to reach an agreement. The lawyer who plays too many games destroys the deal and does not adequately represent her client.

Developing arguments or justifications for each position, you should visualize not only your position but the response from the other side and your reply/rebuttal to that response. Those visualizations will be the bases for your arguments and justifications. Negotiating involves verbal exchanges (discussion, argument, etc.) that justify the merits of the position you take. It is your job to try to persuade the other side that it is in its best interest to agree rather than to litigate or walk away from the transaction *and* to agree to your pending proposal. Thus, the process of *thought* that you went through to develop the interests, compromises, and/or demands/offers to be put forth during the negotiation becomes the basis for the justifications (arguments) that you will assert during the negotiation. Exchanges can be positive or negative. *Positive exchanges* involve those that suggest a desire to accommodate all parties' interests and may also develop a pleasing working relationship between the negotiators. *Negative exchanges* involve those that are designed to intimidate the other side. Negative exchanges may create a positive relation of respect or awe, but they may also further a kind of litigiousness that is often destructive to a successful negotiation.

At this point, it is useful to consider the most likely result of the negotiation process. This involves a detached analysis of where it appears most likely that you can reach accommodations and conclude an agreement. In an economic case, it is a monetary figure. In a more complex negotiation, it is a mix of money and accommodations.

Once you have finished the above preliminary planning, you must then decide how to approach the process of the negotiation dialogue (how to reach the "goal" identified above, or a better result for your client). This involves identifying, at the least, the following:

1. Opening position. You must know how you will start negotiations. This issue incorporates 1) what you will offer and ask for, and 2) how to proceed.

On the issue of *what* to start with, the obvious alternatives to consider are:

a) Starting with more than you want, leaving room for concession and compromise. Even if this is a sham (meaning that you are prepared to offer more than your first position), it is probably the most often taken opening position. It reflects both the competitive aspects and the psychological aspects of the interpersonal relationship that is a negotiation. The competitive aspect is the desire the get the best deal for your client and the fact that negotiations start without the complete exchange of information. Thus, you know what your client would agree to, but you do not know what the other side is prepared to offer. The "psychological" aspect is the desire of all to appear to "give only when they get." Everyone might believe that Christmas sales are reductions on recent markups, but they work none the less.

b) Starting with your best offer, reflecting real accommodation on your side. The trick is trying to sell it to the other parties because it involves a risk that no matter how accommodating you are, the other side will view it as an artificial position that will be changed.

c) Mixing and matching a) and b), above.

Be prepared to listen and accept or adapt the positions of the other party. He may have a solution that is "better" (more likely to achieve an acceptable agreement for all parties) than those that you are suggesting. Negotiating is not about winning; rather, it is about agreeing. Everyone wins when the parties have come to a mutually acceptable agreement.

On the issue of *how* to start, the obvious alternatives include:

- Make your opening offer first.
- Wait for the other party to make the first offer.

2. Concessions. If you have decided to start by demanding more than you may agree to at the end of a successful exchange, you must plan:

- what your second, third, etc., positions will be, and
- the circumstances that will induce you to move from your present position to these fallback stages.

3. "Walk-away" point. Negotiations succeed, but they also fail. Further, the negotiation process may involve more than one meeting. Therefore, you must be aware of your client's final position at this point in the process. It is, of course, obvious, that, a) the client may not wish to pre-determine what will be acceptable, and b) further contact with the client may lead to changes in this position. But before the start, you must know the client's bottom line.

When you are determining the bottom line with your client, you must also be aware of the alternatives that the client will face if the negotiations fail. It is the examination of the alternatives that informs the decision of whether there is a walk-away point, or, whether to set it prior to the start of the negotiations. In some setting, any agreement is better for the client than no agreement.

Implementation of the Negotiation Plan

Careful listening. The most critical factors in the act of negotiating is careful listening to the other party. Cues from the other side will help you determine what arguments to make and how much emphasis to put on each argument. Verbal cues will indicate when concessions are necessary for parties to come to an agreement. You must actively listen to the verbiage, tone, and substance of the other party's statements to sense a willingness to change or a sensitivity to the values that are being presented.

Create a negotiating relationship. The tone, verbiage, and interest in and respect for the statements of the other negotiation (or the appearance thereof) contribute to the kind of relationship that will prevail between the parties. All negotiations involve creating a relationship. Successful negotiations generally are based on a working relationship. The kind of relationship will depend on the interest of your client, your personality, and the personality and interests of the other side, among other factors. Remember that the negotiation relationship, like all relationships is two sided. You may try, but you may not be able to achieve the relationship you desire with the other party. Working relationships range from respectful or friendly to intimidating and fearful. Of course, two homilies should be remembered in considering the relationship that will be most effective:

- "You can catch more flies with honey than with vinegar."

- "What works, works."

CORE DOCTRINAL CONCEPTS CONCERNING CHILD CUSTODY

Definitions—Child Custody

1.   In any action or proceeding brought for a divorce, the court shall enter orders for custody and support as, in the court's discretion, justice requires, having regard to the circumstances of the case and of the respective parties and to the best interests of the child.

2.   There is no prima facie right to custody. Either parent may be awarded custody of the child. There are no set factors by which a court may determine custody. It is up to the court, given the particular circumstances of the case; the parties; and the needs of the child.

3.   A custodial parent who is awarded "physical custody" of a child or children pursuant to a valid agreement between the parties or by an order or decree of a court shall have the child or children permanently and they shall legally reside with that parent.

4.   A parent who is awarded "decision-making authority" of a child or children pursuant to a valid agreement between the parties or by an order or decree of a court shall have the ability to make decisions regarding the health, education, and welfare of the child or children. A court may award decision-making authority to either or both parents. A parent does not have to be the "custodial parent" to be awarded decision making authority.

5.   "Joint Physical Custody" means that both parents have a shared legal right to reside with the children.

CHILD CUSTODY NEGOTIATION PROBLEM

The Slovins have agreed to attempt to resolve all of their disputes over custody through negotiation. The negotiation process has been a lengthy one. During the negotiations, many issues have been resolved but several remain. The trial upon the matter of custody is imminent, and this proximity has encouraged the lawyers to make one last effort to resolve the remaining problems.

The partners who have been handling the matter have substantial experience in matrimonial custody matters. They are certain that in this case, as in almost all custody cases, the litigation leading to a judicial solution (and the judge's order) might be disastrous for the children and for either or both parties. It is obvious to the lawyers that the parties will have to be educated about the legal and practical realities of the dispute so that they can come to a resolution that will be in the best interests of the children.

Fortunately (or unfortunately) for the parties, the partners who have been conducting the negotiations are now engaged in a protracted trial. They cannot conduct these final prehearing negotiations. You have been assigned the Slovin matter. To enable you to manage the negotiations, a summary of the basic background facts of the family and the positions the parties have taken appears below.

The partners suspended the negotiations and had extensive meetings with their clients just before they became involved in their pending trials. In these discussions, they obtained the vital *authorization*, without which there could be no change in the client's demands.

Background Facts of the Family and the Pending Custody Dispute

Family Circumstances

1) The children have been attending PS #6. It is considered to be one of the best public schools in Nita City. After the fourth grade, public school students enter Everson Middle School. There have been several assaults at that school, and at least one murder on the school property (although not during school hours). Everson Middle School does not have the educational reputation of PS #6, and it is undeniably in a far more dangerous neighborhood than PS #6. Most of the children's friends will go to the Elite School starting with the fifth grade. It is a very competitive school. Many of its graduates go on to attend the top Ivy League colleges.

2) Two years ago when Michael moved out, he bought a comfortable home in the same school district. During the two-year separation, the children have been splitting their time between the two parents. The arrangement has been informal, depending on the schedule of the parents. Although the division has been irregular to accommodate the Rita's work schedule, the kids spend about half of the time with each parent. The parents set a schedule, but it is often changed. Michael shares the house with his girlfriend, Linda Allen. She stopped officially working as the children's nanny when she moved in with Michael. Linda is very involved with the children when they are at Michael's. She routinely helps them with homework and takes them to the theater, museums, and the zoo. She is twenty-six years old.

3) Rita Slovin still works until at least 7:30 several nights a week. It is unlikely that she will be able to significantly change her schedule. When the kids were very young, she often was unable to get home until after they were asleep. She, however, never works on weekends so that she can be with the children. She is very politically active in liberal politics. She has "political" problems with organized religion. She was a very good college athlete in track.

4) Michael Slovin had a traditional religious training in his childhood.

5) Loren Slovin is ten years old. She is in the fourth grade. She is a superb gymnast. Every coach has identified her as having potential to make the United States Olympic team. She trains for two hours per day, five days per week. Last year, she went to gymnastic camp for eight weeks in the summer. Although it is impossible to tell whether she will actually make the Olympic team, it is certain that without this level of training she will not have any chance. She wants to do everything, but she seems to be isolated and has little contact with other children outside of her school and organized activities.

The court-appointed psychologist (Dr. Judy), who examined her for the purpose of the custody determination, wrote that Loren says that she feels that her father is the primary caregiver in the family, but she has a strong bond with her mother as well. Indeed, the psychologist has found that since the parents separated there has been more tension between Loren and her father, while she has grown closer to her mother.

6) Sasha Slovin is six years old. He is a very active child who is something of a discipline problem.

Prior Negotiations

A) Negotiated Agreements

The *parents* have agreed that:

1) The custodial status of the children (physical custody and decision making) should be joint. Whatever custody agreement is reached has to be the same for both.

2) Financial arrangements will not have any role in the determination of custody.

The *attorneys* have conceded that:

1) Based on the child care history, the work history, and the attachments of the children, it is unlikely that either spouse would be given exclusive physical custody or right of sole decision making. They also agree that the result cannot be predicted because Rita's refusal to permit Sasha to take prescription medication might weigh in favor of Michael's gaining exclusive decision making. On the other hand, Michael's relationship with Linda might weigh in favor of Rita gaining exclusive physical custody.

2) Based on the same factors, it is generally understood that a court-ordered visitation schedule would give the noncustodial parent significantly more contact than alternative weekends and one month in the summer. The attorneys, however, cannot predict exactly what visitation would be ordered if there is no agreement between the parties.

3) There is no agreement among the attorneys as to how the court would rule on giving Sasha Ritalin.

B) Pending Demands of the Parties

Michael

He insists on having the sole right of decision making unless Rita agrees that:

1) He have custody of the children for at least six of their ten-week summer vacation so that he can take them to their ancestral home to enhance their language and cultural development. He has demanded the last part of July and the month of August.

2) The children be put in private school after the fourth grade.

3) Sasha be put on Ritalin.

4) Rita refrain from indoctrination of the children that poisons them against him and Linda.

5) He have the right to be with the children on religious holidays, Thanksgiving, Christmas, and spring break.

6) If Rita agrees to these conditions, Michael proposes that the children split each week between the two homes: Thursday through Saturday would be spent with him, and Sunday through Tuesday would be spent with Rita. Wednesdays are to alternate.

Michael's reasons for these demands have been set forth during the negotiations:

1) **Summers**. He insists on religious and language training and familiarity with their ancestral home because he feels that his children will otherwise lose "their cultural heritage." He strongly believes that familiarity with the language and the religion is the best access to one's ancestral culture. Thus, he wants them for six weeks of the summer. The month of August is his slow period—schools are closed and there is little consultation work and patients are on vacation—which means that there is little chance that his "time" will be interrupted.

2) **Schooling**. He insists on private school because he grew up in an urban environment and is very concerned about the dangers of children living in Nita City.

3) **Ritalin**. He insists on Sasha receiving the suggested medication because he feels that his son is "in trouble." He feels that Sasha's scholastic and attention problems need immediate treatment before they destroy his life. He feels that Sasha is being injured by Rita's refusal to give him necessary medical treatment.

4) **The prohibition concerning "lifestyle" indoctrination**. He has established a regular and intimate relationship with Linda Allen. She now lives with him. They are committed to each other but have no plans to formalize their relationship after his divorce. Linda no longer works. She has a good relationship with the children and would delight in caring for them. Rita has to get used to this reality.

5) **Vacations**. He has made arrangements so that he can avoid work obligations during the children's vacations. He feels that because Rita's schedule is so much more predictable (as one of the owners of the company, she is her own boss), she should work around Michael's schedule. The specific arrangements that he has made are as follows:

   a) Michael has been going skiing in Aspen at his mother's condo every Christmas for many years. He has never gotten along with Rita's family and, thus, did not go to her family reunion. He wants the kids to go with him. He thinks this is a perfect family activity.

   b) Because he is making a substantial income, he wants to buy an interest in his brother's house in Paris so that he, Linda, and the kids can spend April in Paris.

   c) He feels that Rita's hostility to religion should be honored by her yielding all religious holidays to him, by default. He also thinks that the children will learn to respect their heritage by observance of these holidays.

6) **Custodial division**. He feels that this will maximize the stability in the kids' life. They will quickly get used to the regular rotations and be comfortable in both homes.

Rita

She insists on having the sole right of decision making and exclusive physical custody unless Michael agrees that:

1) Sasha be sent to at least eight weeks of the summer vacation at a rigorous sports camp and that Loren attend an eight-week gymnastics camp.

2) The children stay in a public school.

3) Sasha not be on Ritalin.

4) Visits with Michael be limited to periods during which Linda is not at the "children's second home."

5) Rita have the right to the children for Christmas, Thanksgiving, and Easter.

6) If Michael agrees to these conditions, then Rita proposes that the children split the year between them—six months each. During her six months (August through January), the children spend alternative weekends with Michael, etc.

1) **Summer camps**. She insists on sports and gymnastics camps for the children because she is overwhelmed with the athletic potential of her daughter Loren and is committed to giving her every opportunity to develop her skills. She feels that Sasha's problems can be abated by aerobic exercise. She insists that he attend a sports camp as "treatment." She believes that sports teach discipline and that aerobics induce endorphins, which have great curative value.

2) **Public school**. She is adamantly opposed to private school education because it is elitist and because private schools do not provide the "experience in diversity needed for survival in the twenty-first century."

3) **Ritalin**. She is against medicating children. She feels that ADD is a diagnosis that is made to ease the life of teachers by turning children into zombies. The fact that her son can spend hours watching a movie or playing Nintendo has convinced her that his school problems are the school's problems.

4) **Lifestyle**. She is outraged by the fact that Michael cuckolded her and is "living and sleeping with that nanny in front of the children." She feels that Michael is setting a terrible example for the children. Although she works hard, she expects to devote herself, as much as possible, to the care and protection of the children from such sordidness. She further has made it clear that she believes that Michael will engage in sexual activities either in the presence of the children or in such a manner that the children will be fully aware of them.

5) **Vacations**. She insists on having the children for vacations because of the important family events in her family they will participate in and the support and stability such family associations will make in their lives. The traditional family events are as follows:

a) Her family has an annual reunion during Christmas at her aunt's home in Massachusetts. This week-long event in now attracts her immediate family, children, and many aunts and cousins. She clearly wants custody every Christmas so that the kids can participate in this event.

b) As a child, Rita was taken to Miami every Easter. She wants the kids for the Easter vacation so that she can recreate this experience.

c) Rita has had Thanksgiving dinner at her house every year since she married Michael (twelve years). She often made substantial professional sacrifices to arrange the time to order the supplies and instruct the cook and serving personnel. She can't tolerate not continuing this tradition with her children.

6) **Custodial division**. She proposes a six/six split because of her inability to trust Michael on two counts. First, she feels that under any other type of split, he will dump the kids on her whenever he has a cooking or language class or wants to play tennis. His disinclination to do anything but indulge himself was a major part of the reason for their separation. Now that he is working, things are even worse. During the past two years, he has frequently failed to keep his agreement to take the kids on certain days, and even weeks, because of "obligations." She found out that one of these "obligations" was taking Linda on a weekend vacation. Second, with a less rigorous split she feels that it will be impossible to make sure that Linda Allen is removed from Michael's home. With a six-month split, however, she feels that Michael will have to get Allen a separate apartment. She wants the children to be with her from August through January because then she would not lose any of "her" time with them during the post-Christmas debt collection season.

MODULE 3

TRYING THE EQUITABLE DISTRIBUTION CASE

Facts Concerning Equitable Distribution

Excerpts from Michael Slovin's Statement

Excerpt 1

I am thirty-nine years old. I have a PhD in special education from Nita University. I got the doctorate in YR-10. I also have both a BS and an MS in psychology from Nita University. I went to Choate and Brown before that. I met Rita at school in YR-11. She was in college. She graduated in YR-10. We were married in YR-10, during the spring semester. She and I got our degrees a few months after the marriage. I worked as a special education teacher after we were married. I made a salary of $30,000 per year from YR-10 until YR-9. Rita started working in her family's business as soon as she got out of college. She always made a very good salary (up to $200,000 in YR-1) and got an annual shareholder's distribution of $100,000 as well. She has a minor job in the company but is well paid because she owns it. Her draw of profits is small because of the terms of the partnership agreement. That agreement contains a provision in which she said, "I was really getting more than I should in light of how much my brother George does and how little I do." She has always said this about her role. I am sure she could have gotten a bigger draw if her work was more important to the company's success.

I stopped working full time a year after Loren was born (December 8, YR-10) so that I could be at home and give the baby the nurturing she needed. I spent all of my time with Loren. In YR-8, we moved into a new house, at 400 Schoolhouse Lane, Nita City, Nita, that was big enough for children.

We bought the house for $1 million. Rita borrowed the money from the company. George gave her a 1 percent loan. When she got the money, she put it into our joint bank account. We have paid all of the expenses of maintaining the house with our joint money. The new roof, the taxes, the plumbing, the decorating expenses all came from our joint money. Rita now says that she didn't borrow the money. I know she did. I even have a copy of the loan agreement. I don't know where the signed one is. It used to be in with our papers. The last time I looked it was gone. The copy I have was one that I put with my patient notes by accident. I guess that it would be gone, too, if anyone had known where it was.

Excerpt 2

I started working part time shortly after Sasha was born, in November YR-6. I started a consulting business (Special Needs R Us) for physically and developmentally disabled children. Before Rita and I separated, I carried about a ten-patient load and earned no more than $25,000. I spend approximately eleven to twelve hours per week working. I have had to turn down many patients and several consulting arrangements because the time commitment that work would have required would have prevented me from performing my primary job, which has been parenting.

Excerpt 3

When I left Rita's house on December 16, YR-2, I moved to 92-08 Bellage Boulevard, Nita City. Linda and I and the kids live there. My father owns the house. I picked the Bellage Boulevard residence so that the children would be able to stay in the same school and see their mother. I was able to buy the house from my father because he gave me a purchase money mortgage. He has also helped me with money to furnish the place.

Excerpt 4

I am presently self-employed as a consultant, and I also have a private therapy practice. Since Rita and I separated, I have worked hard to expand my practice. This has taken me away from the children, but I have been earning a little more than $40,000 a year from my consulting and therapy practice. I have gotten a job offer in Aba, Nita. I have arranged to commute from my home so that the children will not be removed from their friends and from the opportunity to visit their mother. I will make $155,000 a year supervising a research project on child disabilities for the Everflash Institute. It is a great opportunity for me. I expect that my income will exceed $250,000 during the two years of the grant that will support the research project, because I will be able to continue my consulting business as well. In fact, this significant position with Everflash will lead to a much more robust private practice, since a psychologist's business directly relates to his reputation.

Excerpt 5

Rita is now trying to destroy my business. In February YR-1, I started to build up my practice so that I had ten regular patients, each of whom saw me once or twice a week, in addition to my work for Everflash. By the end of YR-1, all but one of those patients had left me. The loss of patients is, of course, normal, as people recover. However, I have been unable to replace them because of the terrible lies that Rita has been spreading about me.

Excerpts from Rita Slovin's Statement

Excerpt 1

I am now thirty-three years old. I met Michael while I was in college. He was a lot older than I, and was getting a graduate degree. He was a teaching assistant in my psychology class. We hit it off immediately. He was very understanding. He seemed so mature and caring. We dated for two years and got married immediately before I graduated in YR-10.

Before he died, my father built a very successful business that he called Perfect Toys. He initially manufactured seasonal toys and notions. After a while, however, United States manufacturing costs became too high and he manufactured abroad. When he died in January of YR-10, the business was valued at $10 million. My brother George, who is fifteen years older than I am, took over. George has done a wonderful job. The value of the company is now about $20 million.

The company's management consists of my brother George, who is president; my mother Sylvia, who is vice president and secretary; and me. I am treasurer. I have a twenty-five percent interest in the company. My mother has a forty percent interest, and George has a thirty-five percent interest. Those percentage interests were not our idea. My father had come up with the percentages before he died. He did not want anyone to have a majority interest. He each left us a portion of the company in his will and instructed his lawyers to draft a shareholder's agreement and a stock purchase agreement, which set forth each owner's interest and value of each share, respectively.

I do not see any of that corporate income, other than a $100,000 annual draw. The rest just appears on my return pursuant to IRS regulations. That is what our accountants tell me. I know that not one penny of the company's earnings, other than the salary I draw as head of collections, gets into my bank account. I earn $200,000 a year. I have a title as head of our collections department. The shareholder's agreement we signed when I became of age gave each of us the right to renegotiate profit distribution terms every ten years. I couldn't ask for more money, however, because I just don't do that much.

My job has been to collect money from recalcitrant purchasers. Although collecting money is important, the total amount has never more than five percent of our gross in any year. I am overpaid for my work. I am sure it is because I am the boss's sister. The reason I do not have to do much as collections head is that my brother has supplied me with a fabulous team of managers. They keep meticulous computerized records of our accounts. Our customers generally pay on time, which means that my department does not have to sweat much. However, whenever one of our customers forgets to pay, our computer "tickler" system, which Mensa Gold, the chief administrative officer for the company, designed, prints out an alert sheet and automatically sends a follow-up bill to the delinquent customer. Ninety-nine percent of the time, payment immediately follows.

Even though I work for the company and am a twenty-five percent owner, I can take no credit for the company's increase in value or in its wonderful reputation. My brother has been in total control of production and sales. We have great relationships with our customers—in fact, even with our suppliers. We're a small operation, but a stable, established one. That is why people like to do business with us.

During our marriage, I lived and still live at 400 Schoolhouse Lane, Nita City, Nita. I was able to buy the house because of my income, and the $1 million I received in YR-10 from a distribution of assets generated by the sale of the company's manufacturing plants. The house is 5,500 square feet. There are five bedrooms, an office, a playroom, a family room, living room, eatin kitchen, and a large finished basement. The home is on the shore in a very wealthy community. I bought the home at a bargain price in July YR-8.

Excerpt 2

We fought a lot during the last four years. Michael had started a small business but didn't work at it. He is very talented and could easily make over $100,000 per year. He just doesn't want to work. Even though he was making about $25,000 and I was making $200,000 plus my stockholder's draw of $100,000, by YR-3 his expenditures were taking us over our budget. Our sex life virtually disappeared. During YR-2, I don't think we had sex more than three times. It became obvious to me that I was the worker ant and he was the grasshopper. I began to doubt my values. It didn't make sense that I did all the work while he was loved by all and did nothing.

On December 15, YR-2, despite my increasing anger at his distance from me, I realized that he was right. He was doing just what he wanted to with his life. I, on the other hand, was slaving over collecting money from greedy companies. I had just had a miserable day. I had spent the entire day with lawyers. When I got home, I told Michael that I couldn't stand it anymore. I was going to quit. We would sell the big house and live on his income and my distribution. He told me that I was crazy. He said he couldn't live like a pauper. I told him that after ten years of living off me, he could go to work if he wanted. I said that we could live on our combined—albeit lower—incomes. The next morning, Michael started a fight and walked out on me.

Excerpt from Linda Allen's Statement

Excerpt 1

Michael's father had agreed to let Michael rent a house that he owned at a very reasonable rent so that Michael could move in there. He set this up because he knew that he and Rita were coming to an end. We moved in there with the kids. That night was the first time we were intimate.

When we first started living together, I was very excited about it and the wonderful work that Michael was doing. He got a great job and developed a big private practice. He was throttled by Rita so that he was not able to spend the time on his practice. He could have done this earlier, but he told me about how much consulting work he had to turn down because of Rita, to limit how much business he had so that Rita wouldn't use his success as a reason to get out of giving him his share of their joint money. Before moving out, he said, "It would cost me too much money if I took these clients. I have to wait until I get my divorce." It was all because of Rita and his concern that she would cheat him.

Excerpt from Tommy Friel's Statement

Excerpt 1

I am forty-five years old. I work for Rita Slovin as the assistant manager of the collection division. She is the manager. She has done a wonderful job. She started right out of college. I have a master's in business administration and was upset when she was put in a superior position. I soon learned, however, that she is a natural. The company is stable, but had not grown in profitability in the decade since the founder died. The company's problems were created when the founder died and Rita's brother George took over. He sold off our manufacturing plants and switched to a system of having overseas contractors do all of our manufacturing. This, unfortunately, raised our costs significantly. After he sold the plants, the company's growth stopped because of a serious cash-flow problem that prevented the accumulation of the capital necessary for expansion into foreign markets. George had really made a major problem for the company because he not only sold the plants but he also made the $4 million netted from the sale of the property available to the shareholders. I don't know if he distributed it or, as someone in the legal department once told me, put it into lines of credit that could be drawn upon in thirty-year, callable low-interest loans. All I know is that the money was not available for corporate use. Without this money, the company had a cash-flow problem. It was caused by delay in payments. We were averaging 18 months in collection on accounts of over $100,000. There were very few deadbeats. Our regular accounts had simply learned that they could take advantage of us. This meant that we had to finance our cash-flow needs. It was a serious drain. When Rita took over she solved the problem in less than a year. I haven't been able to figure out exactly what she did. I finally decided it was just the force of her personality that impacted on our customers. The result is that ninety-five percent of our accounts pay within thirty days. We are an industry leader in this regard. Rita has never recognized the importance of her accomplishment. She feels that she just made a few calls and did nothing. She feels that she has been given a minor job because of her lack of training and is overpaid. She is completely wrong.

EXPERT REPORT OF ROWENA MARKS
(ACCOUNTING EXPERT FOR RITA SLOVIN)

I am a partner in the accounting firm of Denton and Turk (D/T), which is the largest accounting firm in Nita, and indeed in the continental United States. We have over 400 accountants in the Nita office alone. I received my BA in accounting from Nita University in YR-20. I went to graduate school and received an MBA from the Wheaton School of Business in YR-17 and a PhD in management and statistics from the Harvard Graduate School of Business in YR-11.

I have been with D/T since I received my MBA. I became a partner in YR-11. I specialize in forensic accounting. I lecture annually to the American Society of Accountants on developments in the field of forensic accounting.

For those who are not familiar with that practice, forensic accounting is the "science" of examining an entity to determine its worth. The term "entity," as it is used in the field, refers to either a business or a person. The evaluation involves an analysis of the entity's present financial structure, its business relationships, its cash flow, its liquid and structural assets, its development, and its potential. I study how a financial situation evolved and identify the factors that contributed to a financial success or failure. I review all documents that reflect the financial data of the subject. Those documents range from personal and corporate tax returns, financial statements, bookkeeping records, and audits to personal bank accounts. After I gather the documents, I carefully examine the entity's financial health. Based on Generally Accepted Accounting Principles (GAAP), I come to a conclusion about a present value for the entity. Corporate valuations are used in many circumstances ranging from sales to stock offers. Forensic accounting, however, is used primarily in litigation contexts in which the value of the subject I am examining is in dispute.

I have been hired as a forensic accounting expert by many people over the past ten years. Most of the people who hire me are involved in complex matrimonial litigations, in which valuations of businesses are crucial to determine the equitable distribution issues of the matter. Eighty-five percent of my clients are husbands.

I was hired by Rita Slovin's attorney to value Rita Slovin's marital property. That property includes Rita Slovin's interest in Perfect Toys, the marital residence, and her interest in Michael Slovin's graduate degree and social worker's license and business.

Perfect Toys

Rita Slovin owns twenty-five shares of stock in Perfect Toys. It is a closely held corporation. There are 100 shares of stock. Her interest in Perfect Toys amounts to $5 million, which is twenty-five percent of the total value of the company. I arrived at the number based on the following factors.

Perfect Toys is a closely held corporation. For those who are unfamiliar with the term "closely held corporation," that type of corporation is one in which the all of the shares of a corporation are owned by a small number of people. Many family businesses are organized in this manner. All of the shares of Perfect Toys, for example, are owned by the wife, son (George), and daughter (Rita) of the founder. Such businesses are generally incorporated because of tax advantages available to those who do business through a corporate entity. The value of the shares is controlled by a shareholder's or stock purchase agreement. The terms and conditions of the agreement, as well as the incorporated valuation formula, must conform with Internal Revenue Code regulations regarding closely held corporations.

Valuing any ongoing business differs from the valuation of property. Property is a static asset whose price varies with the general market. Business values are more dynamic. Their value is based on the expectation of profit in the future through use of the tangible and intangible assets of the entity. Simply, a business's value depends on how profitable it is likely to be. Thus, anticipated future net earnings are the critical factor in business valuation.

Two methods are often used to value a closely held corporation. Both are methods of predicting anticipated profitability from prior business activities. The first is the Gross Earnings Multiplier approach. The second is the Net Earnings Multiplier approach. The Gross Earnings approach involves taking the gross revenue and multiplying it by a 2½ percent number. The 2½ percent multiple is a simple means of incorporating tangible asset and "goodwill" values to the actual income. This method is not widely used because it can give a rather unrealistic and sometimes wildly inaccurate representation of a business's financial health. Many times, a business's gross revenues are high, despite the fact that high operating costs and tax expenses have prevented it from being profitable. Thus, profit is the only accurate basis on which to assess the value of an ongoing business.

The Net Earnings approach involves taking the net income, after taxes, and multiplying it by ten. The ten-times multiple enables an analyst to compare the profit potential of investing in the company against other potential investments. The ten-times multiple assumes that an investor would not buy a business unless it would produce a profit greater than that obtainable through more secure investment. If the yearly profit is multiplied by ten, the investor knows that the investment will yield an annual ten percent profit. This is the best method for evaluating the worth of an ongoing business. Of course, even this test must be adjusted for the specific circumstances. If a Perfect Toys type of company were to be sold, for example, the goodwill generated by relationships that the operating family had with suppliers and customers would vanish. The ten-percent multiple would, therefore, have to be reduced to reflect the reduction in anticipated profits caused by the loss of goodwill. However, goodwill is not a factor in evaluating a company in an equitable distribution context because the company will continue to benefit from the same management.

I valued Rita Slovin's interest in Perfect Toys based solely on the net profits. For the following reasons, the Gross Income approach would be particularly inappropriate as a method for evaluating Perfect Toys. Perfect Toys is a thirty-year-old company, which manufactures educational toys. It is a stable company and has a good reputation in the market for quality products. Unfortunately, the company has not had real growth commensurate with its gross revenue growth since its founder, Rita's father, died ten years ago. Rita's brother, George Tiel, does not have the organizational skills of his father. When George took over in YR-10, the company had a net profit of over $1 million. Gross revenues for that period averaged from $8 to $10 million. Those revenues were extraordinarily high for such a small, family-run business.

However, since that time, the company's costs and resultant gross income have grown. Although the company always made a profit, the ratio of profit to gross sales has gradually decreased during the period of George's control. An examination of the company's financial records reveals that the company has changed to its detriment. Rather than rely on the structure that led to company's prosperity when managed by his father, George sold the manufacturing plants that the company owned and distributed the proceeds to each of the shareholders in YR-10. Rita Slovin's share was $1 million. George has relied on the existing structures. As a result, Perfect Toys increased its gross sales, but has lost profitability. Increases in price have neither been sufficient to match the increase in manufacturing costs nor maintain the company's market share.

Perfect Toys also lavishly compensates its employees. The company provides yearly cost-of-living increases, fully paid health plans, and hefty yearly bonuses across the board, from custodial to managerial employees. The company's employee favorable policies engender loyalty and trust among all who work there. The policies have also contributed to the decreasing gross to net profit ratio. Total net profits have not exceeded $2 million in any of the last five years, despite a gross sales record of $45 million in YR-2. The profit figure is reflected in the company's fillings and is reflected in individual tax returns filed by Rita, her brother, and her mother. Thus, under George's management, gross income rose from $10 million to $45 million. This is a multiple of 4.5 times. Net income, however, only increased from $1 to $2 million. Thus, the gross income cannot be used as a measure of the profitability of the company. A purchaser would not pay a multiple of the gross income because that would not guarantee a profit on the investment. Therefore, Rita Slovin's ownership interest is twenty-five percent of $20 million, or $5 million.

However, that sum is not part of the marital estate. To determine the value of a marital estate, "separate property" must be deducted from present assets to determine the marital property. All assets a) belonging to a spouse prior to the marriage, b) inherited during the marriage, or c) acquired with separate property during the marriage are separate property. Separate property is also the profits created by the investment of separate property if those profits are passively acquired therefrom. The company was worth $10 million at the time of Rita Slovin's father's death and before her marriage. Thus, half of the value is incontestably separate property. Thus, $2.5 million of the value of her shares cannot be marital property. The subsequent increase in value (the remaining $2.5 million) is solely due to the exceptionally good sales efforts of George and the sales staff. Rita has had no involvement in sales and, thus, no responsibility for the increase in value of the company. The increase in value is passive increase for the purposes of evaluating marital property. The $1 million distribution in YR-10 is also separate property in that it is merely the transformation into cash of the inherited stock. The fact that Rita Slovin left the money in a corporate account until she needed it to purchase the house does not change the legal title to the asset. She owned the cash at the time the distribution was announced in YR-10 and has owned it ever since. The mere transformation of the form in which the asset is held from corporate property to cash does not turn it into marital property.

None of the value of her ownership interest in Perfect Toys is an asset of the marriage.

All of her interest in Perfect Toys is separate property.[5]

---

5. Rita's ownership interest is separate and apart from the position she holds in the company and the salary and yearly bonuses she receives. The yearly bonuses are considerable, and have ranged from $50,000 to $75,000 a year. She now earns $200,000.

The Marital Residence

The marital residence is a 5,500 square-foot residence located at 400 Schoolhouse Lane. It was purchased eight years ago by the Slovins. The purchase price was $1 million. Rita Slovin paid for the house out of her separate property. Thus, the first million dollars of this value is merely the transformed value of the separate property. The only part of the value or the house that could be a marital asset is the $500,000 increase in value that has occurred during the period of the marriage. However, that increase in value is passive. Passive increases in value are not attributable to the marriage. The increase is due to market forces that raised the value of all property and was not due to the any insight or enhancement, or improvements paid for with marital funds. Thus, the house cannot be assessed as an asset of the marriage for the purpose of equitable distribution. I have made no assessment of its present market value.

Mr. Brucker's opinion that the marital residence is an asset of the estate worth $2 million is unsupportable. First, the house was bought with separate property from a stock distribution, not with loaned money.

Second, if the money was a loan, the notion that a million-dollar loan (a sum that is a debt and has to be repaid) is an asset worth $1.5 million is absurd. Although the alleged 1 percent interest rate was low, a loan is a debt, not an asset. Third, even if the money was to be treated as a below-interest loan, Mr. Brucker's use of a five percent interest rate to determine the amount of money necessary to produce an annual payment of $75,000 is incorrect. Five percent is the rate statutorily mandated to be used to adjust jury verdicts, but it is not the rate used by professionals to assess the value of money. The appropriate rate should have been ten percent. (Using the ten percent rate, the estimated value would have been $750,000.)

Third, the increase in value of the property due to inflation is the most obvious type of passive accumulation. The house was bought with money loaned exclusively to Rita. Michael has no obligation to repay the money and no ownership interest in the house. The increase in value was due to its purchase, by Rita, with the loan. That loan is separate property, and so is the house.

Michael Slovin's License and Degree

Michael Slovin has a BS and MS in psychology and a doctoral degree in special education from Nita University. He is licensed to teach in special education programs throughout the state. He received his license upon graduation from Nita University. At the time of the marriage, Michael was earning $30,000 a year as a special education teacher. He has just accepted a position as a special education consultant at a salary of $155,000. Although he has not been working full time for the past nine years, it is safe to conclude that he had an earning capacity for the entirety of the marriage.

To determine Michael's earning capacity (not what he actually earned, but what a person with his education, training, and experience can earn), it is necessary to determine his earning capacity in both the public and private sector. The public sector is important because many individuals with PhDs in special education work in the public school system. The private sector is important because Michael's training and degree give him the potential to establish an independent business as a consultant.

I have conducted an examination of salary scales of special education teachers in Nita and in New Haven, where Michael plans to move. I have examined the salary increases for the past ten years for those teachers with Michael's academic and professional credentials. Although Michael started out earning $30,000, my research reveals that special education specialists, in which category Michael must be placed, were in much demand starting in YR-6 because the federal government, and subsequently state governments, allotted funding for physically and developmentally disabled children throughout the country. As a result, more and more special education teachers were needed to fill new positions made possible by the increased federal and state funding. The concomitant result was a shortage of professionals and higher salaries for special education consultants. Therefore, a person with Michael's credentials would now earn $85,000 in the Nita School District. However, a public employee's compensation is not limited to salary. There are many valuable fringe benefits, such as medical insurance, pension payments, and sick and vacation days. The value of these fringes in the Nita School District totals $15,000. This number has to be added to the salary to determine his accurate earning capacity. Thus, his earning capacity in the public sector is $100,000 per year.

I also have analyzed Michael's earning capacity in the private sector. I have done so in light of Michael's present job and his successful part-time consulting business during the past few years. I have gathered salary statistics from the field and have examined similar consulting businesses that are conducted as full-time operations. The results of my research are as follows.

A private sector consultant with Michael's academic credentials and professional background earns from $150,000 to $225,000 in today's market. My research shows that a typical consultant is hired by a particular school district to assess and develop special education programs and is paid an hourly rate of $500 an hour (from a low of $400 to a high of $600 per hour). There is an elite group of professional consultants that receives $500 to $600 an hour. Had Michael pursued his business full time and had he begun it several years earlier, his experience and credentials would have put him in the elite group earning bracket. That conclusion is borne out by an examination of the curricula vitae of the higher earning professional consultants. To be fair to Michael, I have not imputed this income. He has been out of the market because of the joint decision that he should stay at home and care for the children. Further, consultancy is a business with the income fluctuations of all such businesses. Thus, I have reduced the minimum average income of similar consultants ($150,000) by one-third, to compensate for these uncertainties. As a result, Michael's earning capacity in the private sector is $100,000.

Under the applicable law in Nita, Rita is allowed to claim that Michael's potential earning capacity based on his degrees and license is a marital asset that can be valued and divided. The law clearly considers both a degree and a license as an asset. However, the law also "merges" the two separate assets if a substantial amount of time has passed since the acquisition of these separate assets. Consequently, I have imputed Michael's earning potential as a merged asset of the value of his degrees and license. His earning potential is calculated based on the statistics I have detailed above.

Although he will actually be earning $155,000 per year, I am assuming a conservative earning capacity of $100,000 per year. But, the value of the ability to earn $100,000 per year is far greater than that sum. For valuation purposes, the earning potential created by Michael's merged degree and license constitutes a business. As such, the business must be valued at its ongoing business value. As with Perfect Toys, the best method for calculating this value is to determine how much an investor would spend to purchase the ability to make a net of $100,000 per year. The Net Income approach should be used to produce this value. Multiplying the net income by 10 yields a total value to the marriage of $1 million.

The total value of this asset to the marital estate is $1 million. This sum is the value of Michael's business, his license, and his degree. He should compensate Rita for fifty percent of that value ($500,000).

INDIVIDUAL ASSETS

Rita

<u>Separate Property</u>

Shares of Perfect Toys	$5,000,000
House	-$1,500,000
Loan	-$1,000,000
<u>Rita's Marital Assets</u>	$0

Michael

<u>Separate Property</u>

Business/License/Degree	-$1,000,000
Michael's Marital Assets	-$1,000,000

Value of Rita's marital share owed to her by Michael

$1,000,000 x 50%   = $500,000

CURRICULUM VITAE

Rowena Marks
9 Bonneyfield Lane
Nita City, Nita 09999

Academic Background

YR-20   BA, Nita University

YR-17   MBA, Wharton School of the University of Pennsylvania

YR-11   PhD, Harvard Business School

Professional Background

YR-17 to YR-11   Associate, Denton and Turk, Nita City, Nita

YR-11 to date   Member, Denton and Turk, Nita City, Nita

Appointments

YR-10 to date   Lecturer, American Society of Accountants
                       Forensic Accounting Institute

YR-8 to date   Chair, Forensic Accounting Section
                       American Society of Accountants

YR-6 to date   Secretary
                       Nita Accountants Association

Publications

Dissertation: *American Financial Principles in the Twenty-First Century*, Harvard Business School, YR-11

Pamphlet: *Finding the Money*, American Society of Accountants, YR-7

Accounting Archeology: A Source Book for Forensic Accountants, Nita University Press, YR-4

Honors

YR-5   Florida Award for Excellence in Teaching, Gorganza Institute
              Nita City, Nita

EXPERT REPORT OF ALAN BRUCKER
(ACCOUNTING EXPERT FOR MICHAEL SLOVIN)

I am a partner at Foresight, PC, a firm devoted solely to forensic accounting and consulting. I am the founding member of the firm. There are ten members of the P.C. and fifteen associates. We all have accounting and law degrees. I received my accounting degree from Nita University in YR-32. I became board certified in YR-30. In YR-28, I entered Nita University School of Law and received my JD in YR-25. I worked for one of the "Big Eight" accounting firms, Sperry-Hartman-Segal, in the litigation support group. While at SperryHartman, I managed to get my MBA in business management. I stayed at Sperry-Hartman for ten years and was made a member of the firm in my last year there.

I left Sperry-Hartman soon after I was made a member of the firm to start my own company. I took several of my associates with me. At the outset, we specialized in litigation support services for financial disputes. I am often asked to act as a "neutral" forensic accountant in various complex matrimonial litigations. A "neutral" is a forensic accountant whose objectivity is accepted by the both parties.

I have reviewed Dr. Marks's evaluation of the three marital assets at issue in this matrimonial dispute, to wit: Rita Slovin's ownership interest in Perfect Toys, Michael Slovin's degree and license, and the marital residence. I disagree with Dr. Marks's conclusions as to the value of each of those entities.

Perfect Toys

Dr. Marks has concluded that Rita Slovin's twenty-five percent ownership interest in Perfect Toys is worth $5 million and that it is not a part of the marital estate. These conclusions are fatally flawed by two errors. The first is Dr. Marks's reliance on the Net Earnings formula. The second is her failure to accurately assess the importance of Rita's work to the development of Perfect Toys.

As a preliminary matter, the asset value of the company cannot be used as a basis for computing its present worth because the company sold its manufacturing plants and now commissions manufacture of its designs by other companies. The asset value of the company is only $2 million. The only assets are a small office building and the current inventory. The inventory is small because the use of overseas contractors permits the company to produce its goods on an as-needed basis.

Dr. Marks's use of the Net Earnings formula, however, leads to a serious undervaluation of the company. That formula completely ignores the value of both a company's goodwill and its income stream. It assumes that a company has no value beyond its present net profits. Nothing can be farther from the truth. Closely held corporations, such as Perfect Toys, are eminently saleable entities, in large part, due to their favorable and well-established reputations in the marketplace. Goodwill is a highly valued asset. Similarly, cash flow is the hallmark of potential future profits.

The ten times net approach is particularly unacceptable given today's markets. Under that formula, companies such as amazon.com would have no value because they have never had a net profit. Such a result is absurd.

The Gross Revenues formula permits valuations to reflect both the present income and the future potential of a company. The approach permits a general value that is derived from gross sales.

My research, based on an examination of forensic expert valuations in complex financial disputes, has concluded that in the litigation contexts, a 2½ multiple of gross earnings is the best method for evaluating a company. The 2½ multiple of gross income reflects the value of the company's goodwill, inventory, cash flow, capital assets, and growth potential.

I do agree with Dr. Marks that the net revenue base, rather than a gross revenue base, is more reliable in the valuation of mature companies that operate in inelastic markets. However, her use of a net profit approach to value Perfect Toys is inappropriate because the low profit-to-earnings ratio of the last few years seems to be the result of poor management and, therefore, might be improved under new management. The history of the company indicates that under prior management the gross-to-net ratio was under ten to one. There is no reason to think that new management can't restore that ratio. Thus, the company's value cannot be accurately drawn without assessing the enormous profit potential in the income stream as reflected in gross revenues.

Using a Gross Revenues approach to valuing Rita Slovin's twenty-five percent ownership interest in Perfect Toys produces a total company value of $100 million. The company's gross revenue is $40 million annually. Those revenues should be multiplied by 2½ percent. The total value of the company is, therefore, $100 million. Rita's twenty-five percent interest in the company is worth $25 million.

In evaluating the marital estate, however, I agree with Dr. Marks that the value acquired by Rita prior to the marriage must be deducted. The value at that time was 2½ times the $10 million gross ($25 million). Her twenty-five percent interest was worth $6.25 million. That amount should be deducted from the present $25 million valuation. The part of her interest that is a marital asset is, thus, $18.5 million.

Dr. Marks's view that none of Rita's present interest in the company is a marital asset is incorrect. It is based on a superficial analysis of Rita's role in the company's development. It is unsupported by the facts. The president of Perfect Toys, Rita's brother George, was able to generate a dramatic increase in total sales by using borrowed money to expand advertising and production capacity. The loans were only possible because Rita's rehabilitation of the collection practices of Perfect Toys created an income stream that was accepted by the banks as evidence of the stability of the company. This income stream was the collateral for the loan. The loan money would not have been available without her dramatic reduction in the collection period. Without Rita's revolution in the collection department, the income stream would not have been reliable enough for the company to get the loan money that fueled its expansion. The increase in the company's value is founded on her work. It is certainly not the result of passive accumulation. The company could not have generated the money by mortgaging its physical assets because George sold those in YR-10 and distributed the $4 million proceeds, in low-interest callable loans, to the shareholders. Rita Slovin's share was a $1 million loan at 1 percent interest. Thus, the only source of the funds that generated the vast increase in value in this company was the result of Rita Slovin's work.

The full $18.5 million increase in value should be attributable to the marital estate.

Michael Slovin's Degree

Dr. Marks's conclusion that Michael Slovin's merged license and degree is worth $1 million is errone-ous and is based on an unreliable method of valuation.

Dr. Marks makes several incorrect important assumptions. First, she definitively states that Michael would have received the top salary of $85,000 (plus $15,000 in fringe benefits) as a special education teacher in the public sector. That conclusion is not borne out by the available data. While, hypotheti-cally, a person with Michael's credentials could earn that amount of money, in reality, only five percent of those teachers working in the Nita School District earn the top salary. Ninety-five percent of those with comparable credentials to Michael earn less. According to the Nita School District regulations, salary is not solely based on credentials. That top salary is merit based. The top salaries are awarded by a combi-nation of seniority in the particular school, not in the district, and recommendations by supervisors and peer reviews. Since Michael has never worked in the school system in Nita, a conclusion that he would receive the top salary is too speculative. His income, as a public sector employee, must be calculated at the entry-level salary. Entry salary is $30,000 (plus fringes of $10,000 equals $40,000).

Second, Dr. Marks improperly speculates as to Michael's earning capacity in the private market. Michael has never earned more than $25,000 in practice. It is speculative to value his earning capacity at an amount greater than anything he has ever earned. Further, the reference to his forthcoming employ-ment with the Everflash Institute is completely inappropriate. That job was not acquired until after the marriage. It is a temporary, two-year position and cannot be the basis for evaluating his earning capacity.

Michael's degree and license merge into his business. That business produced a net revue of $25,000. Because the starting salary in the public sector is higher ($30,000 plus $10,000 in fringes equals $40,000), that figure should be used. The value of the business is two times the potential gross revenues, or $100,000. Indeed, Dr. Marks final error is to use a "ten times net" rather than the "two times gross" technique to value a license. A license cannot be purchased and, therefore, cannot be valued on a "yield" basis.

Marital Residence

The value of the marital residence is an asset of the marriage. The present value of the house is $1.5 million. The increased value has been caused by the strong real estate market.

The house was purchased in YR-8 for $1 million. The money came from a loan to Rita that was de-posited in their joint account. Both of the marital partners placed their income in this account. The loan was made during the marriage and is a debt of the marriage. By purchasing the house with this money, the house became a marital asset. Further, by using that joint account to make tax payments on the house, both Michael's and her income were used to maintain the loan. Joint payment made the loan a joint asset.

Dr. Marks's view that the house has no value to the marriage is incorrect. The home is worth $1.5 million. The $1 million debt of the marriage to Perfect Toys, Inc. must be deducted. This leaves the $500,000 increase of value as a marital asset. The property was bought with loaned money, which is a marital asset, and maintained with marital income. Rita's and Michael's income during the marriage were an asset of the marriage. Thus, the loan and taxes were paid for with marital assets and the increase in value is a marital asset. The increase in value is one-half million dollars.

Loan

The $1 million loan was at 1 percent interest. This loan was so far below market rate that the value of the difference between market rates and this rate must be considered an asset of the marriage. For the past six years, the prevailing interest rates for unsecured loans in the amount of $1 million have been 8½ percent. Further, it is impossible to imagine that the Slovins would have qualified for a loan. In other words, but for this below-market-rate loan, the Slovins would have had to pay $85,000 per year to maintain the marital residence. The difference between the 1 percent rate and the 8½ percent rate is 7½ percent. The 7½ percent amounted to $75,000. They received the benefit of an annuity of $75,000 every year that they retained the loan. The benefit to the marital estate or this below market loan is 7½ percent of $1 million per year. To determine the value of this annual sum (or annuity) for the six years of the marriage (a loan that is still outstanding), the amount of money needed to generate an annual income of $75,000 must be computed. That value is the amount of money it would take to produce this income. The legal rate for the assessment of litigation costs is five percent. To generate a return of $75,000, $1.5 million would have to be invested at five percent interest.

Thus, the total value of the house and loan to the marital estate is the (present value of the marital interest in the house) minus (the debt) plus (the income value of the unsecured and below-market-rate loan).

House and Loan

Present value	1.5 million
- Debt	1.0 million
+ Loan value	1.5 million
Total	2.0 million

Individual Assets

Rita

Shares in Perfect Toys	25 million
House/loan	3 million

Michael

Business/degree/license	100,000

Marital Assets

Shares in Perfect Toys

25,000,000 - 6,250,000	18,500,000
House/loan	2,000,000
Business/degree/license	100,000

Value of Michael's marital share to be paid to Michael by Rita

$18,500,000

2,000,000

<u>100,000</u>

$20,400,000 - 50% = $10,200,000

CURRICULUM VITAE

Alan Brucker
805 Hoffstot Road
Port Nita, Nita 09998

Education

BA, Accounting, Nita University	YR-32
Certification for Public Accounting	YR-30
JD, Nita University School of Law	YR-25
MBA, Gorganza University	YR-20

Professional Experience

YR-25 to YR-16	Associate, Litigation Support Group Sperry-Hartman-Segal, Nita City, Nita
YR-16 to YR-15	Member Sperry-Hartman-Segal, Nita City, Nita
YR-15 to date	Founder and Senior Member Foresight, PC

Honors

YR-12	Forensic Specialist of the Year, Nita Trial Lawyers Association
YR-10	Commencement Speaker, Nita Graduate School of Business
YR-8	Alumnus of the Year, Nita University School of Law

Exhibits Relating to Equitable Distribution

Exhibit 3

PERFECT TOYS, INCORPORATED
AGREEMENT

between

PERFECT TOYS, INCORPORATED ("Lender") *and* **RITA SLOVIN ("Borrower")**
DATE: 06/28/YR-8

WHEREAS RITA SLOVIN WISHES TO BORROW A CERTAIN SUM OF MONEY FROM PERFECT TOYS, INCORPORATED; AND
WHEREAS PERFECT TOYS, INCORPORATED HAS AGREED TO LEND RITA SLOVIN THAT MONEY; AND
WHEREAS RITA SLOVIN HAS AGREED TO REPAY THAT AMOUNT OF THE MONEY, THE FOLLOWING HAS BEEN AGREED TO:

As of the date of this Agreement, the Lender extends a line of credit in the amount of ONE MILLION DOLLARS ($1,000,000.00) at an annual rate of interest of ONE PER CENT (1 percent) to the Borrower. The line of credit has been established in the Perfect Toys In-House Special Account. The Borrower may draw from that line of credit at any time. The Borrower may repay any amount she draws from the line of credit at her convenience. The note must be repaid, in full, within 30 years from the this date, to wit, by 06/28/YR+22.

TERMS ARE AGREED TO AND ACKNOWLEDGED:

RITA SLOVIN   **PERFECT TOYS, INCORPORATED**
BY:

_____

Exhibit 4

NATIONAL BANK OF NITA

NATIONAL BANK OF NITA, N.A. (BRANCH N-78)

P.O. BOX 5555

CITY ISLAND STATION,

NITA CITY, NITA 99999

RITA SLOVIN AND MICHAEL SLOVIN JTWOS   ACCOUNT : 444449870

670 MOCKINGBIRD SQUARE

NITA CITY, NITA 99907   AS OF 07/06/YR-8

YOUR MONEY IN THE BANK ACTIVITY FROM JUNE 7, YR-8 THROUGH JULY 6, YR-6

CHECKING PLUS

444449870

You began this statement period with a <u>BALANCE OF</u> $62,097.09

You increased funds as follows:

DEPOSITS

3/14/YR-6	$4,098.98
3/15/YR-6	1,000,000.00
3/28/YR-6	4,098.98

You decreased funds as follows:

Got cash from:

3/18/YR-6 #456	2,000.00
3/30/YR-6 #456	2,000.00

Checks paid

3/31/YR-6

Check # 970	1,000,000.00

You ended this statement period with a <u>BALANCE OF</u> $66,294.90

Exhibit 5

PERFECT TOYS, INCORPORATED

Statement of Revenues and Expenditures:
1/1/YR-11–12/31/YR-11

GROSS REVENUES

Sales	$9,120,000	
Commissions\fees\royalties	$460,000	
Contributions	N/A	
Investment income	$400,000	
Other revenues	$50,400	
Total revenues		$10,030,400

EXPENDITURES

Employee salaries	$5,500,000	
Commissions	$130,000	
Rent	$50,000	
Utilities	$10,000	
Materials	$2,300,000	
Office supplies	$30,000	
Advertising	$100,000	
Travel and entertainment	$35,000	
Professional services	$28,000	
Dues and subscriptions	$2,000	
Meetings and conferences	$10,000	
Communications	$40,000	
Insurance	$50,000	
Banking fees	$5,000	
Depreciation	$60,000	
Donations	$200,000	
Taxes	$200,000	
Other expenses	$11,000	
Total expenditures		$8,761,000

Net revenues $1,269,400

Exhibit 6

PERFECT TOYS, INCORPORATED

Statement of Revenues and Expenditures
1/1/YR-2 - 12/31/YR-2

REVENUES

Sales	$41,000,000	
Commissions \ fees \ royalties	$2,800,000	
Contributions	N/A	
Investment income	$400,000	
Other revenues	$1,000,400	
Total revenues		$45,200,400

EXPENDITURES

Employee salaries	$22,400,000	
Commissions	$200,000	
Rent	$920,000	
Utilities	$670,000	
Materials	$10,000,000	
Office supplies	$860,000	
Advertising	$1,800,000	
Travel and entertainment	$240,000	
Professional services	$100,000	
Dues and subscriptions	$35,000	
Meetings and conferences	$78,000	
Communications	$500,000	
Insurance	$1,800,000	
Banking fees	$70,000	
Depreciation	$900,000	
Donations	$1,200,000	
Taxes	$2,000,000	
Other expenses	$38,890	
Total expenditures		$43,811,890

Net revenues $1,388,510

Exhibit 7

RITA SLOVIN
MICHEL SLOVIN

0970

Date 3/31/ YR-6

Pay to the order of M/M D. Ross

$1,000,000.00

One million dollars and 00/100

Dollars

■ NATIONAL BANK OF NITA ■

Rita Slovin

memo

02⬛000089: 444449870" 0100   0970

Exhibit 8

NATIONAL BANK OF NITA

NATIONAL BANK OF NITA, N.A. (BRANCH N-78)
P.O. BOX 5555
CITY ISLAND STATION,
NITA CITY, NITA 99999

RITA SLOVIN AND MICHAEL SLOVIN JTWOS
400 SCHOOLHOUSE LANE
NITA CITY, NITA 99907

ACCOUNT : 444449870

AS OF 06/06/YR-2

YOUR MONEY IN THE BANK ACTIVITY FROM MAY 7, YR-2 THROUGH JUNE 6, YR-2

CHECKING PLUS
444449870

You began this statement period with a BALANCE OF $58,090.89

You increased funds as follows:

DEPOSITS
5/10/YR-2	$500.00
5/14/YR-2	$7,213.33
5/15/YR-2	$500.00
5/28/YR-2	$7,213.33
5/31/YR-2	$250.00

You decreased funds as follows:
Got cash from:
5/11/YR-2 #456	$400.00
5/16/YR-2 #456	$2,500.00
5/30/YR-2 #456	$2,500.00
6/02/YR-2 #456	$400.00

Checks paid
5/14/YR-2 Check #1970	$1,081.89
5/21/YR-2 Check #1971	$234.67
5/28/YR-2 Check #1972	$136.78
5/31/YR-2 Check# 1973	$246.98
5/31/YR-2 Check# 1974	$76.98
6/01/YR-2 Check# 1975	$45.09

You ended this statement period with a BALANCE OF $66,145.16

Exhibit 12

PERFECT TOYS, INCORPORATED
The World's Toy Center

100 TOYLAND AVENUE
NITA, NITA 45678

GEORGE HANOVER, PRESIDENT

December 1, YR-10

Dear Shareholders,

I am delighted to inform you that the recent sale of our aging manufacturing facilities has netted the company a $4 million profit. This permits me to make a one-time distribution of $1 million to each shareholder. This money will be distributed immediately. I have taken the liberty of creating a separate account for each shareholder. Your share of the distribution will be placed in this account and can be withdrawn by you at any time.

I expect that our new five-year plan will lead to a substantial increase in the profits of the company. I would, however, request that you make all efforts to invest the money that you withdraw from these accounts, conservatively. Since ours is a family business, I expect that I will be able to call on each of us to return the money if the company finds it necessary.

George Hanover
President

SUPREME COURT OF THE STATE OF NITA
COUNTY OF DARROW COUNTY

Rita Slovin,   )   Index No.:

Plaintiff,   )

)

against   )   **MEMORANDUM ORDER GRANTING**

)   **A HEARING ON EQUITABLE DISTRIBUTION**

Michael Slovin,   )

Defendant.   )

Dearborn, J.

This is a matrimonial action. The plaintiff, Rita Slovin, has moved for an order declaring that:

1. Her ownership interest in Perfect Toys, Inc. and all distributions from that interest are separate property, not part of the parties' marital estate, and not subject to equitable distribution;

2. The marital residence located at 400 Schoolhouse Lane is separate property, purchased with the plaintiff's nonmarital funds, and therefore not part of the marital estate, and not subject to equitable distribution; and, in the alternative,

3. If this Court were to find that the marital residence were part of the marital estate, the plaintiff's obligations pursuant to a loan agreement, the proceeds of which were used to purchase the subject marital estate, are part of the marital estate and the debt pursuant to that agreement should be equitably distributed.

The defendant, Michael Slovin, has cross-moved for an order that essentially opposes all of plaintiff's requests. He has requested that this Court declare that:

1. The plaintiff's ownership interest in Perfect Toys, Inc., including any appreciation of that interest, is marital property, part of the marital estate, and therefore subject to equitable distribution;

2. The marital residence located at 400 Schoolhouse Lane is marital property, purchased with marital funds, and part of the marital estate, subject to equitable distribution; and

3. The 1 percent interest loan to the plaintiff, Rita Slovin, from Perfect Toys, Inc., is marital property, part of the marital estate, and therefore subject to equitable distribution.

Because of the complexity of the issues, the parties' respective motions cannot be decided summarily. Therefore, **IT IS HEREBY ORDERED** that a full trial be held on the issues set forth above.

SO ORDERED:

Dated: January 12, YR-0

Carlos Dearborn

Carlos Dearborn

CORE DOCTRINAL CONCEPTS CONCERNING EQUITABLE DISTRIBUTION

A. The term "marital property" shall mean all property acquired by either or both spouses during the marriage and before the execution of a separation agreement or the commencement of a matrimonial action, regardless of the form in which the title is held, except as otherwise provided in agreement. Marital property shall not include separate property as hereinafter defined.

B. The term "separate property" shall mean:

1. property acquired before marriage or property acquired by bequest, devise, or descent, or gift from a party other than the spouse;

2. compensation for personal injuries;

3. property described as separate property by written agreement of the parties.

C. Disposition of property in certain matrimonial actions. Except where the parties have provided in an agreement for the disposition of their property, the court, in an action wherein all or part of the relief granted is divorce, shall determine the respective rights of the parties in their separate or marital property, and shall provide for the disposition thereof in the final judgment.

1. Separate property and property acquired in exchange for separate property and the increase in value of separate property shall remain separate property except that;

   a) the increase in value of separate property during the marriage shall be marital property if;

      (1) said increase was directly or indirectly caused by the active involvement of the party having title thereto; or

      (2) said increase was due in part to the contributions or efforts of the party not having title.

2. Marital property shall be distributed equitably between the parties, considering the circumstances of the case and the respective parties.

D. In determining an equitable distribution of property under paragraph C(2), the court shall consider:

1. The duration of the marriage;

2. Any award of maintenance;

3. Any equitable claim to, interest in, or direct or indirect contribution made to the acquisition of such marital property by the party not having title, including joint efforts or expenditures and contributions and services as a spouse, parent, wage earner, and homemaker, and to the career or career potential of the other party;

4. The impossibility or difficulty of evaluating any component asset or any interest in a business, corporation, or profession, and the economic desirability of retaining such asset intact and free from any claim or interference by the other party;

5. The tax consequences to each party;

6. Any other factor the court shall expressly find to be just and proper.

E. In any action in which the court shall determine that an equitable distribution is appropriate but would be impractical or burdensome or where the distribution of an interest in a business, corporation, or profession would be contrary to law, the court in lieu of such equitable distribution shall make a distributive award to achieve equity between the parties. The court, in its discretion, also may make a distributive award to supplement, facilitate, or effectuate a distribution of marital property.

F. The term "distributive award" shall mean payments provided for in a valid agreement between the parties or awarded by the court in lieu of or to supplement, facilitate, or effectuate the division of distribution of property where authorized in a matrimonial action, payable either in a lump sum or over a period of time in fixed amounts. Distributive wards shall not include payments that are treated as ordinary income to the recipient under the provisions of the United States Internal Revenue Code. Under *Jayson v. Jayson*, the Nita Supreme Court held that distributive awards are not taxable events, whereas awards of alimony are, pursuant to the United States Internal Revenue Code.

G. The terms "maintenance" or "alimony" shall mean payments provided for in a valid agreement between the parties or awarded by the court to be paid at fixed intervals for a definite or indefinite period of time, but an award of maintenance or alimony shall terminate on the death of either party or upon the recipient's valid or invalid marriage, or on modification of the agreement or court order.

H. In addition to the disposition of property as set forth above, the court may make such order regarding the use and occupancy of the marital home and its household effects without regard to the form of ownership of such property.

I. In any decision made pursuant to this subdivision, the court shall set forth the factors it considered and the reasons for its decision and such may not be waived by either party or counsel.

MODULE 4

NEGOTIATING THE EQUITABLE DISTRIBUTION CASE

BRIEF OVERVIEW OF NEGOTIATION PLANNING

Structure of Negotiation Preparation

Negotiation preparation requires you to have gone through, at least, the following planning steps, as discussed below:

- negotiation planning and basic strategy;

- implementation of the negotiation plan.

Negotiation Planning and Basic Strategy

Preparation starts with analyzing the "rights-based" strengths and weaknesses of your client's position. You must carefully analyze each of the rights-based issues. Be sure to assess the specific facts of the case when making this analysis.

Continue your preparation continues by identifying the "interest-based" issues and evaluate each such issue. Begin this evaluation by assessing the degree to which each "interest" is shared by the parties and the strength of the commitment of each to that value.

Then move to "strategic gaming."[6] Although the analytic process is similar, the preparatory "gaming" process is simpler in a purely rights-based situation. Gaming in a predominantly *rights-based negotiation*, such as in the equitable distribution problem, means assessing how much each side is likely to modify its economic demands (or offers) to reflect its chances of success at trial—and the value of avoiding the risk of loss at trial.

Gaming in an *interest-based negotiation*, such as in the custody negotiation, requires more complex planning. First, you must identify the differing positions of each party. Second, you must analyze the disputed issues to arrive at potential mutually agreeable accommodations. This is a critical step in planning. While it is true that solutions may develop during the negotiation process and no negotiator should be so wedded to prior planning that an unexpected alternative is dismissed, the best negotiation technique involves identifying a series of potential resolutions prior to negotiation. In thinking about accommodations, you should consider:

- conforming to the client's authorization, which requires substantial counseling (almost negotiating at times) with the client to gain authority for compromises;

- meeting the interests of the other party;

- developing both compromises[7] and/or exchanges.[8]

---

6. Gaming is used to refer to the process of creating, justifying and supporting specific demands that are primarily presented for the purpose of reaching a pre-determined but different result. The "game" of the negotiator is akin to the process of bargaining at a flea market or in the bazaar. Everyone knows that the item will be sold for less than is asked and more than is offered. But, the exact price will only be determined by the skill with which the parties participate in the "game."

7. *Compromises* are changes in position towards a common middle.

8. *Exchanges* are concessions on one or more issues that are made for equal concessions by the other party on other issues.

Third, you must visualize the accommodations (including compromises and/or exchanges) that the other party might propose to the negotiation. In this process, you must construct the potential justifications the other party will use to support the reasonableness of its accommodations.

Warning: Do not let the joy of "game playing" destroy the chances of reaching an agreement. In interest-based negotiations, clients almost always want to reach an agreement. The lawyer who plays too many games destroys the deal and does not adequately represent her client.

Developing arguments or justifications for each position, you should visualize not only your position but the response from the other side and your reply/rebuttal to that response. Those visualizations will be the bases for your arguments and justifications. Negotiating involves verbal exchanges (discussion, argument, etc.) that justify the merits of the position you take. It is your job to try to persuade the other side that it is in its best interest to agree rather than to litigate or walk away from the transaction *and* to agree to your pending proposal. Thus, the process of *thought* that you went through to develop the interests, compromises, and/or demands/offers to be put forth during the negotiation becomes the basis for the justifications (arguments) that you will assert during the negotiation. Exchanges can be positive or negative. *Positive exchanges* involve those that suggest a desire to accommodate all parties' interests and may also develop a pleasing working relationship between the negotiators. *Negative exchanges* involve those that are designed to intimidate the other side. Negative exchanges may create a positive relation of respect or awe, but they may also further a kind of litigiousness that is often destructive to a successful negotiation.

At this point, it is useful to consider the most likely result of the negotiation process. This involves a detached analysis of where it appears most likely that you can reach accommodations and conclude an agreement. In an economic case, it is a monetary figure. In a more complex negotiation, it is a mix of money and accommodations.

Once you have finished the above preliminary planning, you must then decide how to approach the process of the negotiation dialogue (how to reach the "goal" identified above, or a better result for your client). This involves identifying, at the least, the following:

1. Opening position. You must know how you will start negotiations. This issue incorporates 1) what you will offer and ask for, and 2) how to proceed.

On the issue of *what* to start with, the obvious alternatives to consider are:

a) Starting with more than you want, leaving room for concession and compromise. Even if this is a sham (meaning that you are prepared to offer more than your first position), it is probably the most often taken opening position. It reflects both the competitive aspects and the psychological aspects of the interpersonal relationship that is a negotiation. The competitive aspect is the desire the get the best deal for your client and the fact that negotiations start without the complete exchange of information. Thus, you know what your client would agree to, but you do not know what the other side is prepared to offer. The "psychological" aspect is the desire of all to appear to "give only when they get." Everyone might believe that Christmas sales are reductions on recent markups, but they work none the less.

b) Starting with your best offer, reflecting real accommodation on your side. The trick is trying to sell it to the other parties because it involves a risk that no matter how accommodating you are, the other side will view it as an artificial position that will be changed.

c) Mixing and matching a) and b), above.

Be prepared to listen and accept or adapt the positions of the other party. He may have a solution that is "better" (more likely to achieve an acceptable agreement for all parties) than those that you are suggesting. Negotiating is not about winning; rather, it is about agreeing. Everyone wins when the parties have come to a mutually acceptable agreement.

On the issue of *how* to start, the obvious alternatives include:

- Make your opening offer first.

- Wait for the other party to make the first offer.

2. Concessions. If you have decided to start by demanding more than you may agree to at the end of a successful exchange, you must plan:

- what your second, third, etc., positions will be, and

- the circumstances that will induce you to move from your present position to these fallback stages.

3. "Walk-away" point. Negotiations succeed, but they also fail. Further, the negotiation process may involve more than one meeting. Therefore, you must be aware of your client's final position at this point in the process. It is, of course, obvious, that, a) the client may not wish to pre-determine what will be acceptable, and b) further contact with the client may lead to changes in this position. But before the start, you must know the client's bottom line.

When you are determining the bottom line with your client, you must also be aware of the alternatives that the client will face if the negotiations fail. It is the examination of the alternatives that informs the decision of whether there is a walk-away point, or, whether to set it prior to the start of the negotiations. In some setting, any agreement is better for the client than no agreement.

Implementation of the Negotiation Plan

Careful listening. The most critical factors in the act of negotiating is careful listening to the other party. Cues from the other side will help you determine what arguments to make and how much emphasis to put on each argument. Verbal cues will indicate when concessions are necessary for parties to come to an agreement. You must actively listen to the verbiage, tone, and substance of the other party's statements to sense a willingness to change or a sensitivity to the values that are being presented.

Create a negotiating relationship. The tone, verbiage, and interest in and respect for the statements of the other negotiation (or the appearance thereof) contribute to the kind of relationship that will prevail between the parties. All negotiations involve creating a relationship. Successful negotiations generally are based on a working relationship. The kind of relationship will depend on the interest of your client, your personality, and the personality and interests of the other side, among other factors. Remember that the negotiation relationship, like all relationships is two sided. You may try, but you may not be able to achieve the relationship you desire with the other party. Working relationships range from respectful or friendly to intimidating and fearful. Of course, two homilies should be remembered in considering the relationship that will be most effective:

- "You can catch more flies with honey than with vinegar."

- "What works, works."

Core Doctrinal Concepts Concerning Equitable Distribution

A. The term "marital property" shall mean all property acquired by either or both spouses during the marriage and before the execution of a separation agreement or the commencement of a matrimonial action, regardless of the form in which the title is held, except as otherwise provided in agreement. Marital property shall not include separate property as hereinafter defined.

B. The term "separate property" shall mean:

1. property acquired before marriage or property acquired by bequest, devise, or descent, or gift from a party other than the spouse;

2. compensation for personal injuries;

3. property described as separate property by written agreement of the parties.

C. Disposition of property in certain matrimonial actions. Except where the parties have provided in an agreement for the disposition of their property, the court, in an action wherein all or part of the relief granted is divorce, shall determine the respective rights of the parties in their separate or marital property, and shall provide for the disposition thereof in the final judgment.

1. Separate property and property acquired in exchange for separate property and the increase in value of separate property shall remain separate property except that;

    a) the increase in value of separate property during the marriage, shall be marital property if;

    (1) said increase was directly or indirectly caused by the active involvement of the party having title thereto; or

    (2) said increase was due in part to the contributions or efforts of the party not having title.

2. Marital property shall be distributed equitably between the parties, considering the circumstances of the case and the respective parties.

D. In determining an equitable distribution of property under paragraph C(2), the court shall consider:

1. The duration of the marriage;

2. Any award of maintenance;

3. Any equitable claim to, interest in, or direct or indirect contribution made to the acquisition of such marital property by the party not having title, including joint efforts or expenditures and contributions and services as a spouse, parent, wage earner, and homemaker, and to the career or career potential of the other party;

4. The impossibility or difficulty of evaluating any component asset or any interest in a business, corporation, or profession, and the economic desirability of retaining such asset intact and free from any claim or interference by the other party;

5. The tax consequences to each party;

6. Any other factor the court shall expressly find to be just and proper.

E. In any action in which the court shall determine that an equitable distribution is appropriate, but would be impractical or burdensome or where the distribution of an interest in a business, corporation, or profession would be contrary to law, the court in lieu of such equitable distribution shall make a distributive award in order to achieve equity between the parties. The court, in its discretion, also may make a distributive award to supplement, facilitate, or effectuate a distribution of marital property.

F. The term "distributive award" shall mean payments provided for in a valid agreement between the parties or awarded by the court, in lieu of or to supplement, facilitate, or effectuate the division of distribution of property where authorized in a matrimonial action, payable either in a lump sum or over a period of time in fixed amounts. Distributive awards shall not include payments that are treated as ordinary income to the recipient under the provisions of the United States Internal Revenue Code. Under *Jayson v. Jayson*, the Nita Supreme Court held that distributive awards are not taxable events, while awards of alimony are, pursuant to the United States Internal Revenue Code.

G. The terms "maintenance" or "alimony" shall mean payments provided for in a valid agreement between the parties or awarded by the court, to be paid at fixed intervals for a definite or indefinite period of time, but an award of maintenance or alimony shall terminate upon the death of either party or on the recipient's valid or invalid marriage, or on modification of the agreement or court order.

H. In addition to the disposition of property as set forth above, the court may make such order regarding the use and occupancy of the marital home and its household effects, without regard to the form of ownership of such property.

I. In any decision made pursuant to this subdivision, the court shall set forth the factors it considered and the reasons for its decision and such may not be waived by either party or counsel.

EQUITABLE DISTRIBUTION NEGOTIATION PROBLEM

This is a rights-based negotiation. The negotiation is limited to three issues: the value of Michael's interest in 1) Rita's Perfect Toys, Inc., stock, 2) the house, and 3) the loan.

The Slovins have agreed to structure their resolution of their varied disputes over the proper distribution of their marital assets. They decided to deal with the most contentious, and potentially most valuable, assets last. Those assets are Rita Slovin's interest in the closely held corporation, Perfect Toys, Inc. and the combined issues of the family house and loan distribution that was used to acquire it.

The partners who have been handling the matter have substantial experience in such negotiations. Although they recognize that the isolation of the most difficult problems and the decision to work on them last is risky, they agreed that the effort was worth the risk. It is their expectation that once the distribution of the other assets was resolved, the parties would have developed a working relationship that would enable them to compromise over the most contentious issues.

It is obvious to the lawyers that the parties will have to be educated in the legal and practical realities of the dispute so that they can come to a resolution that will be in their best interest. Despite the success of the negotiation on the other assets, the negotiations collapsed. All agreements are pending and could fall apart if this final issue is not resolved. Further pressure has been placed on the parties because the judge has set the trial date on this matter. The trial will start a week from next Monday.

Fortunately (or unfortunately) for the parties, the partners who have been conducting the negotiations are now engaged in a protracted trial. They cannot conduct these final pretrial negotiations. You have been assigned the matter. To enable you to manage the negotiations, a summary of the basic background facts concerning the corporate stock, the house, and the loan, and the positions that the parties have taken on their distribution as a marital asset, appear below.

The partners suspended the negotiations and had extensive meetings with their clients just before they became involved in their pending trials. In these discussions, they have obtained the vital *authorization* without which there could be no change in the client's demands.

BACKGROUND INFORMATION FOR
THE EQUITABLE DISTRIBUTION NEGOTIATION

The Corporate Stock

The asset: Rita Slovin owns twenty-five shares of stock in Perfect Toys. It is a closely held corporation. There are 100 shares of stock. Her interest in Perfect Toys amounts to twenty-five percent of the total value of the company.

Facts Concerning the Stock Asset

1) The *value* of the asset

   a) Deduction of initial value. All parties agree that the value of the company at the date of acquisition must be deducted from the present value to derive the potential amount that could be a marital asset.

   b) Two methods are used to value a closely held corporation. Both are methods of predicting anticipated profitability from prior business activities.

      1) The "gross earnings multiplier" approach involves taking the gross revenue and multiplying it by 2½ percent. The 2½ percent multiple is allegedly a means of incorporating tangible asset, "goodwill" values, and actual income into the estimate.

      2) The "net earnings" approach involves taking the *net* income, after taxes, and multiplying it by ten. The ten-times multiple enables an analyst to compare the profit potential of investing in the company against other potential investments. The ten times multiple assumes that an investor would not buy a business unless it would produce a profit greater than that obtainable through more secure investment. If the yearly profit is multiplied by ten, the investor knows that the investment will yield an annual ten percent profit. Pursuant to this theory, the resulting multiplier is the maximum value of the corporation. It must be adjusted for the specific circumstances. If a Perfect Toys type of company were to be sold, for example, the goodwill generated by relationships that the operating family had with suppliers and customers would vanish. The ten percent multiple would, therefore, have to be *reduced* to reflect the reduction in anticipated profits caused by the loss of goodwill. However, there would be no reduction for the loss of goodwill in an equitable distribution context because the company will continue to benefit from the same management. This conclusion would change if the company had to be sold to make equitable distribution payments.

   c) Value of Rita's shares at the time of acquisition

      1) Using "gross earnings multiplier" theory—equals $6.25 million. It is agreed that the sales in the last year before shares were acquired by Rita Slovin totaled $10 million. Using this theory, the value at that time was two-and-a-half times the $10 million gross yields a value of $25 million. Her twenty-five percent interest was, thus, worth $6.25 million at the time of acquisition.

2) Using the "net earnings multiplier" theory—equals $2.5 million. It is agreed that the net income in the last year before shares were acquired by Rita Slovin totaled $1 million. Using this theory, the value at that time was ten times the $1 million net income, which yields a total value of $10 million. Her twenty-five percent interest was, thus, worth $2.5 million.

d) Present value of her shares

1) Using "gross earnings multiplier" theory—equals $25 million. It is stipulated that the gross earnings of the company are $40 million. Using the gross earnings theory produces a total company value of $100 million. The company's gross revenues of $40 million are multiplied by 2½ percent. The total value of the company is, therefore, $100 million. Rita's twenty-five percent interest in the company is worth $25 million.

2) Using the "net earnings multiplier" theory—equals $20 million. It is stipulated that the net profits of the company are $2 million. Using the net earnings theory produces a total company value of $20 million.

e) Share value subject to equitable distribution

1) Using the "gross earnings multiplier" theory—equals $18.5 million. Her twenty-five percent interest was worth $6.25 million. That amount should be deducted from the present $25 million valuation. The part of her interest in the corporate stock that is a marital asset is $18.5 million.

2) Using the "net earnings multiplier" theory—equals $2.5 million. The company was worth $10 million at the time of Rita's father's death and before her marriage. Deducting that $10 million from the present value of $20 million yields a potential value for equitable distribution of $2.5 million.

2) The *status* of the asset as marital

a) Applicable law. "Separate property and property acquired in exchange for separate property and the increase in value of separate property shall remain separate property except that (a) the increase in value of separate property during the marriage, shall be marital property if (1) said increase was directly or indirectly caused by the active involvement of the party having title thereto. . . ."

b) Rita's position. *None* of the $2.5 million representing the increase in the value of her shares during the marriage is marital property. The increase in value was solely due to the exceptionally good sales efforts of George and the sales staff. Rita had no involvement in sales and, thus, no responsibility for the increase in value of the company. The increase in value is "passive" increase for the purposes of evaluating marital property.

c) Michael's position. The president of Perfect Toys, Rita's brother George, was able to generate a dramatic increase in total sales by using borrowed money to expand advertising and production capacity. The loans were only possible because Rita's rehabilitation of the collection practices of Perfect Toys created an income stream that was accepted by the banks as evidence of the stability of the company. This income stream was the collateral for the loan. The loan money would not have been available without her dramatic reduction in the collection period. Without Rita's revolution in the collections department, the income stream would not have been reliable enough for the company to get the loan money that fueled its expansion. The increase in the company's value is founded on her work and is not the result of passive accumulation.

3) The *percent* of the value of the shares that should be a marital asset. The fact that an asset is a marital asset does not end the inquiry. The exact division of the assets is a matter that requires balancing a variety of factors. The length of the marriage, the means by which the asset was acquired, the means by which the asset was maintained, and the general economic circumstances of the parties are among the factors that can be considered.

4) The ability to pay. The liquidity of the asset: Perfect Toys is a closely held corporation. A closely held corporation is one in which all of the shares of a corporation are owned by a small number of people. Many family businesses are organized in this manner. All of the shares of Perfect Toys, for example, are owned by the surviving immediate family members of the founder. Such businesses are generally incorporated because of tax advantages available to those who do business through a corporate entity. The value of the shares is controlled by a shareholder's or stock purchase agreement. The terms and conditions of the agreement, as well as the incorporated valuation formula, must conform to Internal Revenue Code regulations regarding closely held corporations.

   a) The Perfect Toys, Inc. shareholders' agreement prevents any sale of the stock except to the other shareholders. The sale price is set in the shareholders agreement at 1 percent of the value of the tangible assets of the company at the time of the sale. There are a hundred shares of the company, of which Rita owns twenty-five. Shareholders may only sell to non-shareholders if all shareholders refuse to purchase the stock. The asset value of the company is $2 million. Since 1 percent of $2 million is $20,000, the sale value of the shares under this agreement is, thus, $5,000 (twenty-five percent of $20,000).

   b) It is possible to circumvent this agreement by gaining a court order forcing a sale of the company. Both parties understand that such litigation would be opposed by the company and would be both protracted and costly.

Legal Rules Relating to the Corporate Shares

1) The law relating to the value of the shares. In *Jones v. Jones,* the Supreme Court of Nita held:

   For the purpose of determining the value of property for the purposes of equitable distribution, the prime interest is arriving at a fair and reasonable estimate of present value. In furthering this inquiry, the court should consider all appropriate facts and expert analyses. In light of this purpose, this Court finds that there is no single compilation or analytic theory that can appropriately be used in every situation. Value is a matter for the trial court to determine as an issue of fact.

2) The law relating to the marital status of the shares. Any asset acquired prior to the marriage or by inheritance during the marriage is separate property. But separate property that has increased in value during the marriage will remain separate property unless the increase is due to the active conduct of the party possessing title.

   (1) If the increase in value of an asset that is separate property is due to the *active conduct of the owner*, the increase in value is marital property.

(2) The Supreme Court of Nita held in *Smith v. Smith* that "any significant contribution to the increase in value of separate property is sufficient to render said increase an asset of the marriage for the purpose of equitable distribution."

3) The law relating to the percent distribution of the marital assets. In *Jones v. Jones*, the Supreme Court of Nita held:

The predominant factor in determining the distribution of marital assets is the length of the marriage and the nature of the marital relationship. The parties in this action were married for twenty-one years. The trial court ordered that thirty-five percent of the value of the total marital assets that were in the name of Jonathan Jones be distributed to Jennine Jones. Such an allocation cannot be sustained. After twenty years of marriage, the only equitable distribution is to divide the assets equally.

4) The law relating to the ability to pay. In *Jones v. Jones,* the Supreme Court of Nita held:

When, pursuant to section (E) of the Nita Law of Equitable Distribution, an asset cannot be distributed because such distribution ". . . would be impractical or burdensome, equal assets must be used to compensate." The court stated, "In this action a corporation cannot be sold without great loss of value and other funds do not exist to substitute. The trial court ordered that the unpaid distributive share must be paid in annual payments, which would be taken from the income of Jonathan Jones. Assets equal to the owed, but inaccessible funds must be transferred to Jennine Jones. However, the fixed and automatic deduction from Jonathan Jones's income is inappropriate. During the marriage this asset was not available to either spouse. It was not a liquid asset of the marriage. Once the trial court found that it was impractical or burdensome under Section (E) to transform it into a liquid asset, it would be inappropriate to require Jonathon Jones to transfer a cash equivalent. Once this finding is made, the non-liquid asset of the marriage must be treated as a non-liquid asset of the divorce. Jennine Jones must, thus, receive her distributive share of this non-liquid asset in a non-liquid form. Reversed and remanded. Appropriate distributions would include an interest in the assets of the company or a right to any funds received from a future sale of the company or its assets.

The Home

The asset: Rita Slovin and Michael Slovin own a single family house, 400 Schoolhouse Lane, Nita City, Nita, which was bought with a $1 million cash payment.

Facts Relating to the Home

a) The *value* of the asset

1) Deduction of initial value. All parties agree that the value of the home at the date of acquisition must be deducted from the present value to derive the potential amount that could be a marital asset. The following facts are undisputed.

   (a) Rita Slovin paid $1 million in cash for the home.

   (b) The home is now valued at $1.5 million.

   (c) The source of this money is disputed.

      (1) If the money was a distribution from Perfect Toys, Inc., the initial $1 million of the value of the home would not be an asset of the marriage.

      (2) If the money was a loan to Rita Slovin, the entire $1.5 million would be an asset of the marriage, but the $1 million loan would be a marital debt.

      (3) Thus, no matter how the facts concerning the loan/distribution are decided, the only amount that is potentially a marital asset for the purposes of distribution is the $500,000 increase in value.

b) The *status* of the $500,000 increase in value of the home as marital property

1) It is a 5,500 square-foot house. There are five bedrooms, an office, a playroom, a family room, living room, eat-in kitchen, and a large finished basement. The home is on the shore in a very wealthy community.

2) The home was purchased during the marriage.

3) The present value of the home is $1.5 million.

4) The $500,000 increase in value is due to inflated real estate prices.

5) All tax and maintenance costs for the home have been paid for with checks from a joint bank account. Any income of either spouse was deposited into that account.

6) Rita Slovin makes three intertwined claims: 1) The house was not purchase with marital property but with a cash distribution, 2) the increase in value is "passive," and thus, 3) the increase is not a marital asset.

7) Michael Slovin makes alternative claims. First, he argues that the house was bought with marital property (the loan) and, thus, any increase in value over the debt is a marital asset. Second, he argues that even if the house was not bought with marital property, his contributions to the maintenance of the house through the payment of taxes, etc., transformed the asset into marital property.

Legal Rules Relating to the Home

a) Any loan to either party or to both made during the marriage is a marital debt.

b) Any asset acquired during the marriage through the use of separate property is separate property.

    1) Any distribution from separate property is merely a change in the form of said property and does not transform separate property into marital property.

    2) Separate property that was used to make an acquisition, even if said property is in the name of both parties, becomes a credit to the purchaser.

    3) Separate property that has increased in value during the marriage will remain separate property unless the property has been improved, repaired, or maintained with assets of the marriage.

c) The Supreme Court of Nita held in *Smith v. Smith*:

Any significant contribution to the maintenance or repair of separate property is sufficient to render said increase an asset of the marriage for the purpose of equitable distribution. The trial court's finding that the payment of the mortgage, taxes, utility, and repair bills by Stanley Smith constituted sufficient contributions to transform the property into an asset of the marriage. As a result, the increase in value of that property is an asset that must be distributed.

The Loan/Distribution

The asset: Rita Slovin obtained $1 million from Perfect Toys, Inc.

Facts Relating to the Loan

The *value* of the asset *if it is a loan*

1) Rita Slovin claims that *even if* the money was a loan, it has no value because it is debt that must be repaid.

2) Michael Slovin claims that the loan is worth $1.5 million.

   A) He claims that the difference between the 1 percent interest rate and the prevailing interest rate is the equivalent of a payment of $75,000 a year for the thirty-year life of what he claims to be a loan.

   B) He claims that this $75,000 gain each year should be considered income.

   C) He claims that the present value of that income can be discerned by figuring out how much money would have to be invested to gain a $75,000 per year profit. He uses a five percent return rate. Based on that rate, the annuity is worth $1.5 million dollars ($75,000 is five percent of $1.5 million).

Legal Rules Relating to the Loan

a) There is no Nita statutory or case law concerning the value of a "below normal rate" loan.

b) The statutory interest rate for post-judgment interest in Nita is five percent.

c) For federal tax purposes, a substantial difference between the normal interest rates and the rate of a loan to a taxpayer has been ruled to be income.

d) The Supreme Court of Nita has consistently refused to permit defendants in personal injury cases to introduce proof of the prevailing interest rates because their constant fluctuation.

Prior Negotiation Positions

Rita

- Rita has offered $500,000 for the corporate value.

- Rita has refused to offer anything for the increase value in the house.

- Rita has refused to offer anything for the loan.

Total offer: $500,000

Michael

- Michael has demanded $3 million for the corporate interest.

- Michael has demanded $250,000 for the house.

- Michael has demanded $750,000 for the loan.

Total demand: $4 million

MODULE 5

TRYING THE MARITAL TORTS — BATTERY AND DEFAMATION

STIPULATIONS

The parties have agreed to the following stipulations:

1. Stipulations concerning Michael Slovin's medical condition:

    a. He was admitted to Brookville Hospital on December 21, YR-2.

    b. He was diagnosed as having a systemic streptococcus infection in his arm, which is a life-threatening infection.

    c. Treatment for systemic streptococcus infections may include amputation of the infected limb if the infection cannot be controlled with antibiotics.

    d. Mr. Slovin was treated with a one-week course of intravenous antibiotics in the hospital.

    e. During the first four days of that week, the infection was not responding to the antibiotics and the medical staff started planning for an amputation.

    f. Mr. Slovin had a consultation with an orthopedic surgeon to prepare for emergency amputation.

    g. On the fifth day of hospitalization, blood tests showed a dramatic drop in the level of infection as the antibiotic began to limit the infection.

    h. Mr. Slovin was released on the eighth day of hospitalization, with an oral antibiotic regimen that continued for one month.

2. Exhibit 1 is a fair and accurate representation of the hallway as it appeared on December 16, YR-2.

3. Exhibit 2 is a fair and accurate representation of the house as it appeared on December 16, YR-2.

4. All documents are the originals.

5. The State of Nita has adopted the Federal Rules of Evidence.

INSTRUCTIONS

Battery case witnesses

The trial of the action will be limited to four witnesses:

Michael Slovin

Rita Slovin

Tommy Friel

Linda Allen

Defamation case witnesses

Michael Slovin

Rita Slovin

Anson Able

Victoria Windsor

Linda Allen

Tommy Friel

Allen and Friel may not be called in a bench trial format.

SUPREME COURT OF THE STATE OF NITA
COUNTY OF DARROW COUNTY

Michael Slovin, Plaintiff,	)))	
v.	)	**VERIFIED COMPLAINT**
	)	
Rita Slovin, Defendant.	))	

Michael Slovin, as and for his verified complaint, by his attorneys, hereby alleges as follows:

AS FOR THE FIRST CAUSE OF ACTION BATTERY

1.   At all times herein relevant, the plaintiff, Michael Slovin, and the defendant, Rita Slovin, have resided at 400 Schoolhouse Lane, Nita City, County of Darrow, State of Nita.

2.   On or about December 16, YR-2, at 400 Schoolhouse Lane, the defendant did batter the plaintiff, Michael Slovin, by striking him in the chest and forcefully causing him to slam against a wall.

3.   The plaintiff did not consent to any of the defendant's conduct as set forth in ¶ 2 above.

4.   Upon information and belief, the defendant's conduct, as set forth in ¶ 2 above, was willful and voluntary, and without justification.

5.   As a result of the foregoing, the plaintiff sustained injuries to his head, limbs, and body, and has been caused to suffer severe physical pain and mental anguish as a result thereof; and, upon information and belief, some of these injuries are of a permanent and lasting nature.

6.   The amount of damages sought herein exceeds the jurisdictional limit of all lower courts which would otherwise have jurisdiction.

AS AND FOR A SECOND CAUSE OF ACTION SLANDER

7.   The plaintiff repeats, reiterates, and re-alleges ¶¶ 1 through 4, and ¶ 6, as if fully set forth herein.

8.   That at the time and prior to the defendant's speaking the false and defamatory words concerning the plaintiff, he was an employee of the Everflash Institute and a psychologist engaged in the business of assisting young people.

9.   That on March 21, YR-1, in the presence of Anson Able and Victoria Windsor and several other persons unknown to the plaintiff, the defendant spoke false and defamatory words concerning the plaintiff the substance of which was that the plaintiff had been "taking advantage of a women patient by seducing her."

10.   That Victoria Windsor is and was the dean of the Nita School, a private school in Nita.

11.   That as dean she was in a position to recommend the defendant to the parents of her students who needed therapeutic assistance.

12.   That the import and meaning of the statement was to injure the defendant in his business capacity in that it alleged that the defendant could not be trusted to act in an appropriate manner as a psychologist in the treatment of young patients.

13.   The false and defamatory statement was made for the purpose of depriving the defendant of the good opinion and injuring his professional reputation by deterring Victoria Windsor from recommending the defendant to the parents of her students who needed psychological assistance.

14.   That the defendant's statement was not protected by a qualified privilege, or, in the alternative, that if it was so protected, the defendant abused that privilege and lost its protection by making the statement with malice toward the plaintiff or with a reckless disregard for his interests.

15.   That by the reason of such slanderous publication, the plaintiff was denied such references and incurred a substantial loss of earnings, was subject to contempt and ridicule, was injured in his professional reputation, and has suffered great pain and mental anguish, all to the plaintiff's damage.

AS AND FOR A THIRD CAUSE OF ACTION SLANDER

16.   That at the time and prior to the defendant's speaking the false and defamatory words concerning the plaintiff, he was an employee of the Everflash Institute and a psychologist engaged in the business of assisting young people.

17.   That on March 21, YR-1, in the presence of Anson Able, chair of the board of directors of the Everflash Institute, the defendant spoke false and defamatory works about the plaintiff, to wit that he was "always think[ing] of himself first and how to exploit people for his own benefit so that anyone he interacts with him is at risk."

18.   That the defendant's statement was not protected by a qualified privilege, or, in the alternative, that if it was so protected, the defendant abused that privilege and lost its protection by making the statement with malice toward the plaintiff or with a reckless disregard for his interests.

19.   That as a result of such words the plaintiff's employment has been threatened, injuring his professional reputation and causing him to suffer great pain and mental anguish, all to the plaintiff's damage.

WHEREFORE, the plaintiff, Michael Slovin, demands judgment against the defendant:

1.   Awarding compensatory damages to the plaintiff in the amount of $10,000,000 for the injuries sustained as result of the defendant's willful conduct in battering him;

2.   Awarding compensatory damages to the plaintiff that will fairly and adequately compensate the plaintiff for the injury to his professional reputation presumed to flow from the defamatory statement about the defendant in his professional capacity and for the actual loss of income created by the statements, together with interest thereon and his costs of this action, and for such other relief as the Court deems just and proper.

3.   Awarding punitive damages to the plaintiff in the amount of $5,000,000 for the intentional and malicious battery.

4.   Awarding punitive damages to the plaintiff in the amount of $5,000,000 for the intentional and malicious defamatory statements.

JURY DEMAND

The plaintiff demands a trial by jury in these actions.

SMITH AND SMITH
By

Henrietta Smith
_____

Henrietta Smith
Attorneys for Plaintiff
1212 Court Street
Nita City, Nita 09999

RETURN OF SUMMONS

I hereby certify that the above complaint was personally served on Rita Slovin at her residence at 400 Schoolhouse Lane, Nita City, Nita.

James Smith

James Smith
Reliable Subpoena and Process, Inc.

VERIFICATION

STATE OF NITA   ))
ss   ))
COUNTY OF DARROW   ))

_____

Michael Slovin, being duly sworn, deposes and says:

I am the plaintiff herein and have read the foregoing complaint and know the contents thereof; that the same is true to my personal knowledge, except as to matters therein stated to be upon information and belief, and as to those matters I believe to be true.

Subscribed and sworn to
before me on this 1st day of October, YR-1

Michael Slovin
_____
Michael Slovin

Harry Struck
_____
Notary Public for the State of Nita

SUPREME COURT OF THE STATE OF NITA
COUNTY OF DARROW COUNTY

Michael Slovin,   )
Plaintiff,   )
)
v.   )   **VERIFIED ANSWER TO**
)   **VERIFIED COMPLAINT**
Rita Slovin,   )
Defendant.   )

The defendant, Rita Slovin, by her attorney, in answer to the plaintiff's verified complaint, hereby alleges as follows:

1.   Admits ¶¶ 1, 10, 11, and 16 of the verified complaint.

2.   Denies ¶¶ 2 through 9, ¶¶ 12 through 15, and ¶¶ 17 through 19 of the verified complaint.

FIRST DEFENSE

3.   That the plaintiff's complaint fails to state a claim upon which relief can be granted.

SECOND DEFENSE PRIVILEGE

4.   That any statements alleged by the plaintiff in his second claim for relief were made by the defendant to Victoria Windsor as dean of the Nita School and were made solely in the interests of the school and concerned the health and safety of the students.

5.   That the defendant as a mother of school-age children had the duty and responsibility to inform Victoria Windsor of the fitness of a potential therapist that would be recommended by the dean.

6.   That the defendant's statements were privileged community interest statements.

7.   That the defendant's statements were made in good faith, without any malice or intent to injure the plaintiff.

THIRD DEFENSE TRUTH

8.   That the statements concerning the plaintiff's conduct in establishing an intimate relationship with Linda Allen were true in that the plaintiff admitted that he had spent hours with Linda Allen helping her deal with her emotional problems and, at or about the same time or immediately thereafter, established an intimate relationship with her to the extent of living together.

9.   That any statements alleged by the plaintiff in her complaint to have been made by the defendant concerning the plaintiff are true.

WHEREFORE, the defendant demands that the complaint be dismissed and judgment entered in favor of the defendant and that costs of this action be assessed against the plaintiff and for such other relief as the Court deems proper and just.

WHEREFORE, the defendant demands judgment against the plaintiff:

1.   Dismissing the complaint in its entirety;

2.   Reasonable counsel fees, costs, and disbursements expended in the defense of the counterclaims; and,

3.   For such other and further relief as this Court deems just and proper.

Dated: October 28, YR-1

Attorney for Defendant

Artemis Jones

Artemis Jones

VERIFICATION

STATE OF NITA   ))
ss   ))
COUNTY OF DARROW   ))

_____

Rita Slovin, being duly sworn, deposes and says:

I am the defendant herein and have read the foregoing answer and know the contents thereof; that the same is true to my personal belief except as to those allegations stated to be upon information and belief and to those matters I believe to be true.

Subscribed and sworn to
before me on this 31st day of October, YR-1

Rita Slovin
Rita Slovin

Harry Struck

Notary Public for the State of Nita

STATEMENT OF MICHAEL SLOVIN

1   **Background**

2

3   I am thirty-nine years old. I have a PhD in special education from Nita University. I got the

4   doctorate in YR-10. I also have both a BS and an MS in psychology from Nita University. I went

5   to Choate and Brown before that. Rita started working in her family's business as soon as she

6   got out of college. She always made a very good salary (up to $200,000 in YR-1) and got an

7   annual shareholder's distribution of $100,000 as well.

8

9   I stopped work a year after Loren was born (December 8, YR-10), so that I could be at home

10 and give the baby the nurturing she needed. I spent all of my time with Loren. Things between

11 Rita and me changed when I stayed at home. The most obvious change occurred because Rita

12 didn't think that I spent enough time doing housework. Rita hired Linda Allen a year after we

13 moved into the new house. She was hired in November YR-7. I am presently self-employed as

14 a consultant, and I also have a private therapy practice.

15

16 Since Rita and I separated, I have worked hard to expand my practice. This has taken me

17 away from the children, but I have been earning a little more than $40,000 a year from my

18 consulting and therapy practice. I have gotten a job offer in Aba, Nita. I have arranged to

19 commute. I am making $155,000 a year supervising a research project on child disabilities

20 for the Everflash Institute. It is a great possibility for me. I expected that my income would

21 exceed $250,000 during the two years of the grant that will support the research project

22 because I am be able to continue my consulting business as well. In fact, this significant

23 position with Everflash should have led to a much more robust private practice because a

24 psychologist's business directly relates to his reputation. But it has not grown. My income

25 from my practice is down to an actual $20,000 per year.

1 **Linda Allen**

2

3 Linda Allen and I had no intimate physical relationship before my separation from Rita. Now, of

4 course, we are emotionally and physically intimate. I have had nurturing protective feelings about

5 Linda for a long time. Even before we started living together, I wanted to support her in any way

6 I could. On several occasions, after the children were asleep, I let her sleep in the huge bedroom

7 bed at 400 Schoolhouse Lane because she was emotionally distressed and I didn't think that it

8 was appropriate for her to be alone until she felt more secure, so she did sleep there once or

9 twice. But there were no intimacies. I just let her sleep in my room to protect and calm her. If Rita

10 was in the house and Linda was distraught, I would sit with her in her room until she was asleep.

11

12 Linda is such a wonderful person that her joy radiates. As a result, I enjoy giving her presents

13 as much to see how happy they made her as to thank her for the way she nurtured the chil-

14 dren. A few years ago, I gave her one gift that was a little over the top. It was a birthday gift of

15 a diamond and ruby necklace that cost $1,500. I never specifically told Rita about my gifts to

16 Linda because it was a gift from me, not Rita and me. Rita must have known, however, because

17 Linda wore the necklace all the time.

18

19 Although Linda and I live together, we are very careful to avoid being intimate in the presence

20 of the children. I have kissed and held her in their presence. In fact, we were just kissing when

21 Rita walked in to pick up the kids on March 15, YR-1. We were on the couch in the family room

22 while the kids were watching a DVD in front of us. Rita's story that we were acting improperly

23 is absurd. Linda had just taken a shower, and we were just lying together watching TV while

24 waiting for Rita to come and pick up the kids.

25

26 **December 16, YR-2**

27

28 As the years passed, I became more and more dissatisfied with my marriage. For example, we

29 haven't had sex since YR-3. I was constantly thinking of leaving. I couldn't take it anymore, and

30 on December 16, YR-2, I left.

1   It was a very tense time. The night before, Rita had told me something about quitting her

2   job. I don't remember exactly what she said on the evening of December 15, YR-2, but

3   I didn't believe it for a second. I have been trying to get her to quit or slow down for years.

4   She complained endlessly about the long hours, but it was obvious that she loved the job

5   more than she loved her family. She never would have quit.

6

7   The final blow that caused me to leave occurred on December 16, YR-2. Rita has been

8   having an affair with Tommy Friel. I know that he has a male boyfriend, but that doesn't

9   mean that he can't have sex with women. They always work the same hours, often until

10 11:00 p.m. I am sure that they stopped off for some "quiet time" together on some of

11 those late nights. When Tommy stopped by for his usual ride to work that morning, the

12 two of them stood at the door giggling at each other. Linda was dressing the children in

13 their rooms. I accused them of having an affair. The way they were acting was just rubbing

14 my nose in it. Rita, of course, denied it. Tommy just stood there looking guilty. We shouted

15 at each other for about two minutes. I was standing near the kitchen, and she was facing

16 me on the other side of the hallway. I started to walk away from her to go to the kitchen,

17 and Rita moved in front of me and blocked my way. I tried to get around her, but she just

18 smashed into me. It was like I was some kind of tackling dummy. She lowered her head,

19 and smash! I grabbed her by the shoulders to stop from falling. She acted like I was hurting

20 her, but I only grabbed her to stop falling. I then tried to get her off of me so that I could

21 get to the kitchen. I didn't hold her at all hard. I really just pushed her to one side. Then,

22 out of nowhere, she hit me. She hit me so hard that I was knocked backwards and smashed

23 into the frame of the kitchen door. Both of her arms just came up and whacked my head.

24 I was stunned. I hit my head and my left forearm. If I hadn't twisted around and gotten my

25 arm up in time, the blow to my head could have been lethal. My left arm flew up when Rita

26 hit me. As I fell backwards, it smashed into the corner of the doorway into the decorative

27 bas reliefs on the molding. The impact was about two inches below the left elbow on the

28 outer side. It was a stunning blow. Rita acted as though she was the victim and collapsed

29 into Tommy's arms.

1 I pulled myself together, despite the shock of the blow to my head. I couldn't take it. I told

2 Rita to get out. She told me that she had bought the house and that if anyone was leaving, it

3 was me. I left. Linda packed our things, and I carried them to the car. I wanted to get out as

4 fast as I could. I did not say anything because I did not want to worry Linda or the kids, but my

5 arm was throbbing so much that I had trouble holding the heavy bags. I actually dropped one

6 down a whole flight of stairs.

7

8 Linda and I had been planning to have lunch with at The Homestead. Linda had packed

9 up things for the children's day. I had asked Linda to get the kids' things ready so that she

10 wouldn't be delayed in going to eat. When I left Rita's house, I moved to 92-08 Bellage

11 Boulevard, Nita City. Linda and I and the kids live there. My father owns the house. I picked

12 the Bellage Boulevard residence so that the children would be able to stay in the same school

13 and see their mother. I was able to buy the house from my father because he gave me a pur-

14 chase money mortgage. He has also helped me with money to furnish the place.

15

16 **Damages**

17

18 Rita's attack on me, both the physical and the psychological, has caused me no end of injury in

19 so many ways. First, on the night that she attacked me my forearm swelled up as though my

20 elbow had moved down a couple of inches. It throbbed. I also had a big bump on my head.

21 The swellings went down some with ice. By the third day, however, the bruise on my arm was

22 all red and sensitive. I went to the doctor. She said that I had an infection. I took antibiotics. It

23 didn't get any better. The doctor said that I might have to be hospitalized because I was get-

24 ting a systemic strep infection. I knew that such infections had killed people. The newspapers

25 called it the "flesh-eating disease." I read about a man in Canada who cut himself and got this

26 infection. They amputated an arm and both legs, but he died anyway. I was petrified. Fortu-

27 nately, a month of high-dosage antibiotics stopped the infection. The pills bothered my stom-

28 ach. I had pain for weeks. But the stomachache was better than being hospitalized, so I kept

29 my mouth shut and took the drugs. Second, the injuries caused me to cancel all of my appoint-

30 ments on December 17. One of the appointments I cancelled was with an eighteen-year-old

1   patient (J.K.) who had been developing uncontrollable anxiety attacks about his school work.

2   I had been working with him for months and had talked about his case, at least my concern

3   about his suicidal ideation and the anxiety I felt because of my responsibility to him, with

4   Linda and Rita. I certainly told them that I was so concerned with him that I felt that I had

5   said the wrong word or wasn't there when he needed me we would lose him. He committed

6   suicide because of the cancelled appointment. The day after the appointment, he called me.

7   He told me that he was lying in his tub and had slit both wrists. He said that he wanted me to

8   know that I had come close to pulling him from the brink, but everything had overwhelmed

9   him yesterday and when I wasn't there, his intention solidified.

10

11   He then hung up. I called the police and told them to rush to his home, but it turned out that

12   he had rented a motel room. By the time he was found, it was too late.

13

14   Every day, I think that I could have saved him but for the injury Rita caused. She killed him.

15   It has ruined my life. I have to take medication for my depression. I can't sleep or eat. My

16   weight has dropped to dangerously low levels. My doctor told me that I may have to commit

17   myself if I can't find a way to overcome the anxiety. The depth of despair lasted for over a

18   month. Because of the imminence of the holidays and the age of my clients, Linda was able to

19   reschedule most of my appointments into January. By that time, I was able to work, although

20   I still suffered, and even do today, because of my failure to save J.K.

21

22   Third, she is destroying my business. In February YR-1, I started to build up my practice so

23   that I had ten regular patients, each of whom saw me once or twice a week, in addition to

24   my work for Everflash. By the end of YR-1, all but one of those patients had left me. The loss

25   of patients is, of course, normal as people recover. However, I have been unable to replace

26   them because of the terrible lies that Rita has been spreading about me. She tells people that

27   I abused my female patients. This story has gone viral, and now those at the private schools

28   and many pediatricians no longer mention me to their patients who need counseling. Rita's

29   slanders have caused me to lose almost $80,000 in billings in the last year. I know that the

30   loss of business is caused by those slanders. Based on what Linda told me about what she

1   overheard at the Hofstraconian function, I am certain that Rita has told everyone those lies. In

2   fact, one of the local pediatricians, Bonnie Base, who used to refer business to me, basically

3   said exactly that. She told me that it didn't matter because she was moving to Hong Kong, as

4   her husband was being transferred by his company, but that she had become uncomfortable

5   referring young patients to me because of what was being said. I worked with her for years. She

6   had a lot of adolescent and teenage girls as patients because of her subspecialty in adolescent

7   and teen gynecology.

8

9   The statements hurt me, and I am bringing this defamation suit because they have undoubt-

10   edly hurt my chances to expand my private therapy practice unless they are shown to be the

11   lies that they are. I am particularly concerned because she made these irresponsible state-

12   ments to members of the board of directors of the Everflash Institute who are employing me.

13

14   And it is her proclivity to act in this kind of malevolent manner that causes me to insist on

15   having the sole rights of decision making and legal custody to protect the children.

STATEMENT OF RITA SLOVIN

1   **Background**

2

3   I am now thirty-three years old. I met Michael while I was in college. He was a lot older than I,

4   and was getting a graduate degree. He was a teaching assistant in my psychology class. We hit

5   it off immediately. He was very understanding. He seemed so mature and caring. We dated

6   for two years and got married immediately before I graduated in YR-10. Before my father

7   died, he built a very successful business that he called Perfect Toys. He initially manufactured

8   seasonal toys and notions. After a while, however, United States manufacturing costs became

9   too high and he manufactured abroad. When he died in January YR-10, the business was

10   valued at $10 million. My brother, George, who is fifteen years older than I am, took over.

11   George has done a wonderful job. The value of the company is now about $20 million.

12

13   During our marriage, I lived and still live at 400 Schoolhouse Lane, Nita City, Nita. When we

14   were first married, my marriage with Michael was almost perfect. Michael was supportive

15   and exciting. But things changed. Michael had stopped working because he wanted to stay

16   at home with the children. I worked endlessly because my income had to pay for everything.

17   Our sex life virtually disappeared. During YR-2, I don't think we had sex more than three

18   times. It became obvious to me that I was the worker ant and he was the grasshopper.

19

20   **December 16, YR-2**

21

22   I began to doubt my values. It didn't make sense that I did all the work while he was loved

23   by all and did nothing. On December 15th, YR-2, despite my increasing anger at his distance

24   from me, I realized that he was right. He was doing just what he wanted to with his life. I, on

25   the other hand, was slaving over collecting money from greedy companies. I had just had a

26   miserable day. I had spent the entire day with lawyers. When I got home, I told Michael that

27   I couldn't stand it anymore. I was going to quit. We would sell the big house and live on his

28   income and my distribution from Perfect Toys. He told me that I was crazy. He said he couldn't

1 live like a pauper. I told him that after ten years of living off me, he could go to work if he

2 wanted. I said that we could live on our combined—albeit, lower—incomes. The next morn-

3 ing, Michael started a fight and walked out on me.

4

5 I know that he started the fight on purpose. As I was in the hall bathroom on the second floor

6 checking my hair, I heard Michael talking to Linda in the hallway. They must have been stand-

7 ing right outside of the bathroom. I heard Linda say, "If you are not too busy, how about having

8 lunch at The Homestead?" Michael then said, and I remember his exact words, "I don't think

9 that we will have time. I want you to get our stuff and the kids' things ready, but make sure

10 to watch the entryway when Friel comes to pick up Rita. I may need you." I had no idea what

11 that meant until later.

12

13 On the morning of December 16, Tommy Friel came to pick me up. Tommy picks me up every

14 morning and drives me to work. He works with me. He has been my best friend for the past

15 seven years. He lives a few miles from us. He stops by every morning, and we drive to work

16 together. He also drives me home. I was in the foyer. I opened the door for Tommy. Then I went

17 into the kitchen to get my pocketbook. When I walked back into the foyer to leave, Michael

18 seemed to appear out of nowhere standing in front of the doorway to the kitchen blocking

19 my path to the front door. He stood there and said the most vicious things. He accused me of

20 having an affair with Tommy. That is ridiculous, and Michael knows it. Tommy is gay and lives

21 with his companion, Anthony Smith. Even though the kids were watching from the top of the

22 stairs, he said that I was a tramp and was "screwing" Friel. Michael was vicious that morning.

23 When I heard him demeaning me and Tommy, I realized that this is what he had been planning

24 when he talked to Linda.

25

26 Michael was still blocking my path from the kitchen to the front door. When I tried to walk

27 by him, he moved to block my way with his body. I played a lot of basketball when I was in

28 school. I thought that I could get around him by faking left and running as fast as I could to

29 the right. It didn't work. He was too quick for me. When I bolted to the right, he moved into

30 my path. As a result, I bumped into him quite hard. I had hardly gotten my breath back when

1   he grabbed me. He grabbed my arms so hard that they were pinned to my sides. I tried

2   to twist out of his grip. I couldn't do it. He was scaring me. He looked furious, and he was

3   really hurting me. All my twisting just seemed to make him squeeze harder, although we did

4   move so that we were turned around. I finally thought to try to break his grip by raising my

5   arms out in front of me, towards him. I jerked them up hard, and he let go. When he let go,

6   I stumbled backwards and would have fallen but Tommy had come up behind us and caught

7   me. Michael said that I thrust him into the wall. That isn't true. I know that my hands never

8   touched him. I don't even know if he even hit the wall at all. I certainly am not strong enough

9   to hurl him anywhere.

10

11 I heard that he claims that in some bizarre way of thinking, I am responsible for the suicide

12 of one of his patients. He only had two appointments that day. Since I found that he was fit

13 enough to see his lawyer about getting interim maintenance from me, he certainly could have

14 seen his patient. No wonder he is trying to blame me.

15

16 **Defamation**

17

18 It is obvious that Michael was having an affair with Linda before he moved out. I saw them

19 holding hands on several occasions. Now I am worried about his affair influencing the chil-

20 dren. That is why I seek sole custody. On March 1, YR-1, I walked into his new house to pick

21 up the kids. Despite his insistence on having them, I still take care of them every weekend so

22 that he can "have some time to himself." Michael was lying with Linda on the couch. The kids

23 were sitting on the floor in front of them. It looked like Michael and Linda were having sex.

24 The robe was open so that it lay on the couch on either side of Michael. When I entered the

25 room, she got up very quickly. She wasn't wearing anything under the robe. It just isn't right.

26 I couldn't stand the humiliation. I told Tommy about it, and he shocked me by telling me all

27 about Linda sleeping with Michael while she was working for me. I was so upset that I looked

28 through our old checking records. I know Michael. If he was having an affair with Linda, he

29 would have given her presents. That was when I found the check to Beautiful Baubles for

30 $1,500. I called the store and learned that he had bought a diamond and ruby necklace.

1   I remembered that I had seen Linda wearing one. Then, I knew for sure. I wasn't suspicious

2   before seeing the payment because I thought that her gaudy necklace was paste. Couples

3   separate every day. But nobody has an affair with the nanny in his wife's bed. He could at least

4   have gone to a hotel.

5

6   Until then, I had not realized how emotionally manipulative he is. I think that everyone should

7   know what he does with young vulnerable women like Linda. Everyone who we knew. I felt

8   they should know that Michael could not be trusted. As a result of this, at a function spon-

9   sored by the Hofstraconian Club on March 21, YR-1, I talked to both Victoria Windsor and

10   Anson Able about Michael. When Mr. Able asked me about the children's health, I told him

11   that I was worried because Michael was sharing his bedroom with the children's very much

12   younger nanny and actually letting them see her lying on top of him naked except for an open

13   robe. I also said that I was concerned about the kids because Michael often acts as though he

14   was trying to help them with their emotional problems, as he had with our nanny, but was

15   really seeking personal advantage in our divorce. I also told Ms. Windsor, Mr. Able, and oth-

16   ers at that function that Michael had spent a great amount of time with our nanny while we

17   were still together and that he had explained spending so much time with her because, as he

18   said, "I am just trying to help her become an adult." I told them that I was now certain that

19   he started out helping Linda, but then took advantage of that "helping relationship" to start

20   sleeping with her. I also told them that the second he left me he started sharing his bedroom

21   with her. I never said that Linda was a patient of Michael's or that he could not be trusted

22   with young women. I did, though, ask them what they thought Michael and Linda were doing

23   before he moved out. I didn't talk to anyone else. Mr. Able and Ms. Windsor needed to know

24   about Michael, and Mr. Able asked me. And so, I told them.

25

26   I have to admit that I was pleased that Mr. Able asked because he is the chair of the board of

27   directors of the Everflash Institute. They employ Michael, and Everflash should know what

28   Michael might do with patients. I also know that Ms. Windsor is the dean of the Nita School,

29   which has a student population that might be a source of patients for Michael. I thought that

30   it was important for her to know as much as she could about him for exactly that reason.

STATEMENT OF LINDA ALLEN

1   **Background**

2

3   I am twenty-four years old. I live with Michael Slovin and help take care of his two children,

4   Loren and Sasha. They are wonderful kids. I love them as though they were my own. I have

5   taken care of Loren since she was four years old and Sasha since he was born. I started work-

6   ing for the family in YR-7. I was almost eighteen and had just graduated from high school

7   when I saw an ad for an *au pair*. The ad said that they were looking for a "mother's helper,

8   with some housekeeping." I thought that would be a good way to get out of Sioux Falls, Idaho,

9   so I applied for the job. They had placed ads in local papers in small cities throughout the

10   West. During the interview, I found out that I would actually be a "father's helper." I thought

11   that was neat and took the job.

12

13   **Michael Slovin**

14

15   Michael was very helpful to me. I left home a wreck. I was neglected by my parents. My

16   mother was always at work, and my father was a drunk. I really raised myself. Michael

17   seemed to sense my need. He spent a lot of time with me from the first day I started work-

18   ing. He would comfort me. He made me talk about my home life. He got me to work through

19   my developmental problems. I would often just hold his hand as I was talking about my

20   childhood. Over the years, I realized that I loved him. About two years after Sasha was born,

21   Michael let me see his needs. He opened up to me about how lonely it was to have a wife

22   who didn't understand him. I felt so important to be able to help him.

23

24   Michael gave me presents to thank me for helping him with his problems. He started giving

25   me nice presents. At first, he would give me a blouse or a dress from Bloomingdale's. By YR-3,

26   he was giving me wonderful presents. He gave me presents at Christmas, on my birthday, and

27   Valentine's Day. He gave me a gorgeous necklace, a pearl bracelet, diamond earrings, and

28   other jewelry. I know that the necklace cost over $1,000.

1   We never really had a physical relationship before he moved out. In YR-4, we kissed for the

2   first time. After that, I began to sleep in the same bed with him when Rita was on trips. We

3   never had sex—oral or otherwise. Michael said that it would be wrong. I really respected him

4   for that.

5

6   I know Anthony Smith. On January 3, I talked to Anthony about how much I liked my job and

7   how I felt sorry for my boss, who was unhappy in his marriage. I also told him that I had got-

8   ten a very nice birthday gift from my boss and that I was sorry that I couldn't do anything in

9   exchange. I think he said that I could "give my boss some very personal services." I thought

10   that was a joke. We both laughed. I did not talk to him on March 1, YR-3. I did not even see

11   him on that day because I was away with the kids. March 1, YR-3, was a beautiful day. I took

12   the kids for a drive in the country. We stopped at a town about twenty miles north and had

13   lunch at a little place looking over a frozen pond. I rented skates for the kids, and they skated.

14   We came back just in time for the kid's dinner. I have the receipt for the lunch, but I can't find

15   anything for the skating. I paid in cash.

16

17   **December 16, YR-2**

18

19   Tommy Friel drove Rita to and from work every day. He worked for her. He was quite nice. He

20   would talk to me sometimes when Rita wasn't ready to leave. I think that he had a "thing" for

21   Rita. He was supposed to be gay, but he put the moves on me. He once asked me if I wanted

22   to party with him. When I said no, he said that he thought I would enjoy doing a little cocaine

23   with him and his companion. I knew that he meant a date, though. He was always staring

24   longingly at Rita. Michael told me that they were having an affair. It was obvious.

25

26   On December 16, YR-2, Michael and I were going to have lunch at a very nice restaurant called

27   The Homestead. He had asked me to get my work out of the way early so that we would

28   have time for a nice lunch before the kids returned from school. When Friel came to pick up

29   Rita, Michael couldn't take it anymore. Michael saw them flirting and accused them of having

1   an affair. Friel couldn't deny it. He just hung his head and looked guilty. Rita blew up. I was

2   standing at the top of the stairs with Loren, but that didn't stop Rita. She just screamed that

3   Michael was a sorry excuse for a man and that she wanted him out of her house. After she

4   said that she could "kill him," she, like, ran into the kitchen, where there were knives. When

5   she returned, Michael tried to quiet her. He held her to calm her. She writhed in his arms. She

6   was hitting and pushing at him, but he kept trying to control her. He couldn't. She actually

7   knocked him backwards. I saw her clasp her hands together and bring them up hard and fast

8   under his chin as though she was trying to knock his head off. The blow pushed Michael back

9   so hard that he smashed into the wall. I couldn't see him because my view straight down was

10   blocked, but I heard and felt the thump all the way up on the walkway above the entry. Friel

11   jumped in and grabbed Rita. Loren was confused. She didn't understand what Michael was

12   trying to do. She was crying and saying, "Daddy, stop *hurting* Mommy." After that, Michael

13   told them that he would leave, but that he would have to get a lawyer to see to it that the

14   children were provided for. She said that she didn't care. She meant that she didn't care

15   about him or them. It was awful to hear a mother talk like that.

16

17   I was standing at the top of the stairs because Michael told me that he wanted me to have

18   the kids out of their rooms and ready to leave for school as soon as Rita left. That is why we

19   were up there waiting.

20

21   **Damages**

22

23   After Friel and Rita left, I packed our and the kids' stuff. Michael was still hyper-excited by

24   what Rita had done. Later, he carried everything down to the car. At one point, I heard a series

25   of loud thumps. I was afraid that he had fallen down the stairs. I called out to see if he was

26   all right. He shouted back that I shouldn't worry, that he wasn't hurt. Michael's father had

27   agreed to let Michael rent a house that he owned at a very reasonable rent so that Michael

28   could move in there. He set this up because he knew that he and Rita were coming to the end.

29   We moved in there with the kids. That night was the first time we were intimate.

1   During the night of December 16, Michael was awakened by pain in his arm. There was a huge

2   bump on his left forearm. It was the size of an apple. He said that he hurt it when Rita pushed

3   him. Probably to avoid my worrying, he hadn't said anything about it bothering him when he

4   took the luggage or I wouldn't have let him. But it started to swell rapidly that evening. We

5   put ice on it. It started turning red the next day. He went to the doctor and had to take antibi-

6   otics for a month because he had a serious infection. He was worried that he would lose his

7   arm. I was terrified for him. He was so anxious for so many weeks. Fortunately, the antibiotics

8   stopped the infection.

9

10   The arm got better within a few weeks, but the antibiotics haven't been able to ease his pain

11   over the suicide of one of his patients. Since then he can't sleep or eat. He has lost so much

12   weight that I am afraid for him. He is 5'10" tall and weighed 185 pounds. He is now down

13   to 150 pounds and losing more almost every day. He is taking a lot of anti-anxiety medica-

14   tion. Rita really caused that suicide. Michael had cancelled all of his therapy sessions set for

15   December 17. It was the day after Rita assaulted him. His arm was hurting. He hadn't taken

16   any time off in months. He just felt too drained to give his patients the attention that they

17   needed. One of those cancelled sessions was with the young man who slit his wrists. Michael

18   is so angry with Rita because he is certain that he could have helped the young man get over

19   that crisis. He was so depressed for the first few weeks after the suicide that I rescheduled all

20   of his appointments until January.

21

22   When we first started living together, I was very excited about it and the wonderful work that

23   Michael was doing. He got a great job and developed a big private practice. He was throttled

24   by Rita so that he was not able to spend the time on his practice. He could have done this

25   earlier, but he told me about how much consulting work he had to turn down because of Rita

26   to limit how much business he had so that Rita wouldn't use his success as a reason to get out

27   of giving him his share of their joint money. Before moving out he said, "It would cost me too

28   much money if I took these clients. I have to wait until I get my divorce." It was all because of

29   Rita and his concern that she would cheat him.

1   But ever since his patient committed suicide while talking to Michael on the telephone, he

2   has been unable to function. He can't sleep. He has lost a lot of weight. He really can't func-

3   tion in any capacity, even with me helping. He is just so sad. He feels guilty about canceling

4   the therapy appointment. It is so sad because he really isn't the same person.

5

6   **Defamatory Statements**

7

8   On March 21, YR-1, Michael and I attended a fundraising event for Everflash, his new employer.

9   I heard what Rita said about Michael to Mr. Anson Able, the chair of the board of directors of

10   Everflash. I was standing talking to a friend of mine. We were in the grand meeting room of

11   the Hofstraconian Club. The room was filled with people. There must have been 1,000 people

12   in the room. The sound level was very high. However, as I was telling my friend about an

13   amazing school project that Sasha was doing, I heard Rita's voice. I turned and saw that she

14   was standing behind me in a group that included Anson Able and Victoria Windsor, dean of

15   the Nita School, an elite private school in Nita City. Rita was telling them awful lies about

16   me and Michael. Rita said, and this is an exact quote, "Michael should not be permitted to

17   treat young women, maybe even girls. He can't be trusted if they are attractive. He will act

18   like their best friend. He will use the therapeutic relationship to suck them into an intimate

19   emotional relationship with him. Then right into his bed."

20

21   Mr. Able said that this didn't sound like the Michael whom he knew. Rita then said that all

22   one had to do was see what he did with the nanny, Linda Allen. One day she was a young

23   woman who he was treating for emotional problems, and the next the two were sharing a

24   bedroom. She even said that Michael and I were sleeping together in her house while they

25   were married and while the children were there. I was shocked and hurt. It just wasn't true.

26   But I knew that Michael and Rita were suing each other, and I didn't want to do anything that

27   would make things worse for Michael. So, I told him all about it. He said that we should leave

28   it to his lawyers, and we did.

STATEMENT OF TOMMY FRIEL

1 **Background**

2

3 I am forty-five years old. I work for Rita Slovin as the assistant manager of the collection

4 division. She is the manager. I met Michael Slovin as soon as Rita started working for the

5 company. I also immediately realized that she was wrong to have married Michael. He really

6 was a bum. He had her wrapped around his little finger. As soon as he could, he stopped

7 working. His excuse was to take care of Loren. I pick Rita up and drop her off after work. It is

8 convenient for both of us and makes the drive fun. I have always liked Rita. I am gay and have

9 known so since I was a boy. Rita and I do hug and hold hands from time to time, but that is

10 because she is my good friend. I would never cheat on Anthony. Before I finally admitted to

11 myself that I would never be happy unless I accepted my sexual identity, I tried to go out with

12 women. Years ago, I did have girlfriends. I was pretty successful at establishing friendships

13 with women, but I never felt comfortable with a sexual relationship with a woman.

14

15 **Defamatory Statements**

16

17 A few years after they hired Linda Allen, Michael started an affair with her. I learned all about

18 it from my companion, Anthony Smith. He has often met Linda in the supermarket. They

19 became friendly. She is really an innocent and decent person, but Michael has conned her like

20 he did Rita. She does all of the work, but thinks that he is wonderful. In January YR-3, Linda

21 met Anthony in the store. She did not know that Anthony and I were together. She never

22 used any names, but she confided in him that her boss was "more than a boss" and that "he

23 was miserable in his marriage and was going to leave it as soon as he could figure out how to

24 do it right." She also told Anthony that her boss had given her the most wonderful Christmas

25 present. She said that her present to him had been "very personal services." On March 1 or 2,

26 YR-3, I was again shopping with Anthony. We dropped by the market after work to get a few

27 things for supper. Linda walked right by me and after some conversation with Anthony about

28 the weather, he asked her about her boss. I heard Linda say, "He is so exciting that it is hard to

1   keep my hands off him until 'the wife' leaves in the mornings." Anthony said something that

2   I couldn't hear. I then heard her giggle, and she said, "And how! When he left this morning

3   I could hardly get out of bed." Anthony is an anthropologist. His team got a large grant to fund

4   a multi-year exploration in the northwest quadrant of the Gobi Desert in Mongolia. He left

5   three months ago and will not be back until June YR-1.

6

7   I didn't tell Rita about what Linda said because I thought that she would just get upset at me.

8   She knows that I have never liked Michael. I had often told her that he was a bad apple. She

9   was so deluded by Michael that I feared that she might just "kill the messenger." After she told

10   me about seeing Linda draped all over Michael with hardly a stitch on her, I told Rita about the

11   conversation I overheard between Linda and Anthony. She started to cry and muttered, "I'll

12   make him pay for that, I will. I feel so dirty."

13

14   I am a member of the Hofstraconian Club. I was not at the event of March 21, YR-1. I heard

15   from several members that Rita told everyone about Michael's affair with Linda Allen. I was

16   told that she told everyone that Michael had been and was having an affair with the troubled

17   young woman who was their nanny. She was reported to have said that it was hard to believe

18   that he wasn't having sex with her while she worked for Rita because the second he moved

19   out he installed her in his bed. Many people reported that she said, "If he had any judgment

20   at all he would have gone to a motel," and "I have to get full custody. I don't know if I can trust

21   him with the kids."

22

23   **December 16, YR-2**

24

25   I was at their house on the morning of December 16, YR-2. I expected a scene because Rita had

26   told me that she was going to quit her job, sell the house, and go to law school. I told her that

27   Michael would never stand for that because all he wanted was her money. When I arrived,

28   I got more than I bargained for. Linda was at the top of the stairs with the kids. Michael walked

29   in and started accusing Rita of having an affair with me. Michael acted like he was in a fury.

30   Now that I think back, I believe that Michael was faking the whole fury thing and that he was

1   just trying to set Rita up. He must have been planning to walk out with Linda and the kids. He

2   had to be acting, because he knows that I am gay. He has known Anthony for years. In fact,

3   we have gone to dinner and many events with the Slovins.

4

5   Michael started yelling at me. He called me a "sleazebag" and Rita a "whore." He knew that

6   the kids were watching since all of us could see them at the top of the balcony, but that didn't

7   stop him. When Rita tried to leave, he stepped in front of her and grabbed her. He held her

8   arms against her sides and started to shake her. I thought that he was going to hurt her. She

9   was struggling to get away, but couldn't. I heard Loren shouting, "Daddy is hurting Mommy,"

10   while he was shaking her. I approached them to try to break it up. By then, they had twisted

11   around so that Michael was looking toward me. Seeing me approaching, he suddenly let go

12   and quickly stepped backwards. Rita's hands flew over her head as she tried to keep from

13   falling. I was close enough to hold her up so she did not fall. Michael may have stepped into

14   the wall, but I was busy with Rita and didn't notice. He certainly didn't act as though he was

15   hurt. What he did do was yell at Rita to get out of the house. She told him to leave because it

16   was her house. He said, "I will leave, but you'll be sorry." When we got back from work, the

17   house was empty. She deserves better. She killed herself to be with the kids despite the fact

18   that she worked long hours.

STATEMENT OF ANSON ABLE

1   My name is Anson Able. I am seventy-two and recently retired. I had my own company,

2   Able Investments, for which I did investment portfolio management. I am now involved

3   in public works activities through which I am on several boards of public interest compa-

4   nies. I am the chairman of the board of directors of the Everflash Institute. Everflash is a

5   public interest, not-for-profit company dedicated to improving the lives of young people

6   who are being raised in depressed economic settings. We provide counseling to assist with

7   their ability to cope with emotional, physical, and employment problems. We are presently

8   attempting to expand our ability to assist those who have to combat both the trauma of an

9   economically challenged environment while dealing with physical disabilities.

10

11   Michael Slovin is a very talented therapist who we have hired to supervise a grant that we

12   acquired to develop new therapeutic approaches towards helping those with physical dis-

13   abilities. This is a multimillion dollar grant that will pay for a director and several therapists as

14   well as research assistants. We have funding for three years and hope to get more. Michael

15   has been hired as the project director. Michael demonstrated such a high level of human

16   sensibility during his interviews that he was really the only one we seriously considered hir-

17   ing. He really is a wonderful person. He will be paid a salary of $150,000 a year and be given

18   offices and time to conduct a private therapy practice of up to twenty hours a week. We

19   advertised for the position, and the stated compensation included the salary and our profes-

20   sional estimate of the income that a psychologist with the status of the project director would

21   make in private practice.

22

23   I also know Rita Slovin. She and her family have been significant sponsors of the projects of

24   the Everflash Institute. I also know her personally through a variety of social and professional

25   interactions over many years. Members of her family used to invest with me, but they with-

26   drew their funds about a year ago. Their account was one of my most important accounts.

27   Right after they did, other of my long-term clients also changed their money managers. It left

28   a big hole and hastened my decision to retire. It was galling since Rita's brother and the other

1 clients all used the same excuse, virtually with the same words. They said that they withdrew

2 their funds because I was too conservative, but I knew that Rita's brother was telling everyone

3 they meant that they thought that I was too old.

4

5 My father was one of the founding members of the Hofstraconian Club, and I have been a mem-

6 ber for years. March 21, YR-1, was the date of our annual multi-organization fundraising event.

7 The Club has a fine restaurant and one of the best cocktail mixologists. Part of all our fundraisers

8 features his novelty special cocktails. I had three that were wonders. The mix of alcohols, fruits,

9 and bitters was a wonder. Later, I saw Rita Slovin talking with Dean Victoria Windsor. I joined

10 their conversation. They were talking about a new toy that her company was making. Then

11 Dean Windsor mentioned that there was a terrible flu going around that had decimated her

12 students. I asked Rita about her children. She told me that she was worried about them because

13 of Michael's relationship with their young nanny. She said, "Michael had taken advantage of a

14 young woman patient of his, their nanny, by seducing her and engaging in intimate activity with

15 her in front of the children in her house." I heard her say that Michael "always thinks of himself

16 first and how to exploit people for his own benefit so that anyone he interacts with him is at

17 risk." She told me that Michael had moved out of their house, taking the nanny and moving

18 her into his bedroom. Rita then said that all one had to do was see what he did with the nanny,

19 Linda Allen. "One day she was a young woman whom he was treating for emotional problems,

20 and the next the two were sharing a bedroom." She even said that Michael and Ms. Allen were

21 sleeping together in her house while they were married and while the children were there.

22

23 Divorce is rampant. I was outraged at Rita for using her anger at the breakup of her mar-

24 riage to attack Michael. Rita seemed just like the rest of her family. She should not have

25 been demeaning Michael just because she was angry at the collapse of their marriage. He is

26 a quality person and an excellent administrator and therapist. I talked about this with other

27 members of the board who had heard her slanders. I don't remember which ones, but we

28 did not dismiss Michael, although one or two board members were concerned about his

29 behavior. I eventually explained to them that he was such a wonderful administrator that we

30 couldn't see a way to maintain the grant without him.

1   I was saddened to learn that Michael's private therapy practice has not thrived. Although

2   I have not talked to any of the parents who have or have not hired Michael to treat their

3   children nor personally heard any discussion about Michael that might affect his ability to

4   attract patients, I did hear what Rita said to me and Dean Windsor. That type of stuff always

5   gets around. I am sure that it has been a significant factor in Michael's loss of business.

6

7   I never spread gossip. I do not know how many people heard Rita's statements about Michael

8   taking advantage of women patients. Some may call me cynical, but I don't believe most of

9   what I hear and half of what I read. However, as I already noted, I did talk to several of my

10   friends and colleagues on the board about Michael's conduct. We mostly discussed how a

11   divorce can create enormous hostility.

STATEMENT OF VICTORIA WINDSOR

1   My name is Victoria Windsor. I am the dean of the Nita School, which is a private school

2   in Nita. I have been the dean for eighteen years. Before that, I was corporate counsel for a

3   large university. I left that job when I divorced my husband. I got the divorce on the ground

4   of adultery.

5

6   The school was established almost 150 years ago and has a large and very successful group

7   of alumni who have given generously. Their contributions have been brilliantly invested,

8   not by me, so that we now have the largest endowment of any private school in the coun-

9   try. As a result, we expanded our student population by adding 100 students on full schol-

10   arships. As dean, I am in charge of all budget and teaching issues. I also have taken it upon

11   myself to supervise our student counseling center. In that capacity, I talk to all parents

12   whose children have acted in such a way as to indicate a need for therapeutic counseling

13   in excess of that we can provide. I also assist parents in seeing the need for professional

14   assistance when a child needs it and I try to steer them to appropriate therapists. Many of

15   these therapists have extensive relations with the school, such as assisting with fundraising

16   efforts and in interviewing prospective students seeking scholarships. My decision to rec-

17   ommend certain therapists has caused some controversy. Two therapists whom I refused

18   to recommend claimed that I misrepresented my reasons for making these decisions. I told

19   our board that I had concerns about both therapists unnecessarily extending therapies

20   while they said that the real reason was that they refused to give the school kickbacks in

21   the forms of contributions to the scholarship fund. After all, it is important for the Nita

22   School to play an active role in all aspects of our students' development and therapy is a

23   vital aspect.

24

25   I only recommend therapists whose work is known to me and who have the highest reputa-

26   tions in both their professional and personal lives. I know that some feel that my concern

27   with the personal lives of the therapists is inappropriate, but I feel that how somebody lives

28   provides an insight into his judgment and judgment is the most critical skill that a therapist

1   brings to the therapeutic relationship. I have not recommended Michael Slovin. I have not

2   recommended him because of his lack of judgment. This is a fatal failing in a therapist.

3

4   I had known his family, but I did not know much about him until I heard about him at a func-

5   tion sponsored by the Hofstraconian Club on March 21, YR-1. I was talking to Rita Slovin and

6   Anson Able. Anson seemed to have been spending a lot of time at the bar before we started

7   talking. I had just mentioned a flu epidemic that was emptying my school when Able asked

8   Rita about her children. She said that she was worried about them because Michael was shar-

9   ing his bedroom with their very much younger nanny and actually letting the children see her

10   lying on top of him naked under an open robe. She also said that she was concerned about

11   the kids because Michael often acted as though he was trying to help the kids with their emo-

12   tional problems, as he had with her nanny, but was really seeking personal advantage. She

13   then returned to the topic of Michael living with the children's nanny. I realized that she was

14   angry at their divorce, but I thought what she said about Michael's moving out of the marital

15   home and ensconcing their nanny in his bedroom the same day was significant. She said, "The

16   second he left her [Rita], he started sharing his bedroom with the nanny." She also said, "What

17   do you think they were doing before he moved out?" and "Like he always does, he sucked her

18   in by acting so interested in her emotional problems." When I heard Rita ranting, I assumed

19   that most of the details I had heard from her were not meant to be literally true because of her

20   anger, but I checked it out because a therapist's judgment and lack of self-interest is critical

21   to successful child therapy. I found that Michael did move in with the nanny. This information

22   was central to my decision not to recommend Michael Slovin. When I found that Michael had

23   moved out of his marital residence and immediately established an intimate relationship with

24   his children's young nanny, I realized that his judgment was too poor for me to trust him with

25   my children.

26

27   Anson was obviously angered by what Rita has said. It was as though the statements were a

28   personal attack on him. His face turned red. He literally stuttered when he spoke. He said that

29   Rita and her entire family should be embarrassed at how they were treating Michael because

30   he was a wonderful young man and would never have sex with a patient. Rita actually never

1   said that Michael had sex with a patient or an ex-patient. In fact, she was quite clear that in

2   her opinion he had never had a therapeutic relationship with their nanny. What she said was

3   that he claimed to have had such a relationship as a cover story to hide the fact that they

4   were having an affair.

APPLICABLE LAW: DEFAMATION

The law defines defamation as the publication of a communication to a third person that tends to expose a person to hatred, contempt, or ridicule, or to induce an evil opinion of him or her in the minds of people who hold to normal notions of morality. In this case, the alleged communication(s) were verbal. An alleged defamatory verbal communication is called slander. The plaintiff has no action unless you find that the plaintiff has suffered some specific economic or pecuniary loss called actual damages.

The plaintiff, Michael Slovin, claims that the defendant, Rita Slovin harmed him by making statements that the plaintiff was "taking advantage of a woman patient by seducing her," that the plaintiff was "always think[ing] of himself first and how to exploit people for his own benefit so that anyone he interacts with is at risk," and other similar false and defamatory statements.

To establish that, the plaintiff must prove all of the following:

1. That the defendant, Rita Slovin, made one or more of the above statements to a person or persons other than the plaintiff.

2. That the person or persons reasonably understood that one or more of the above statements was about the plaintiff;

3. That because of the facts and circumstances known to the listener(s) of the statement(s), it tended to injure the plaintiff in his occupation or to expose him to hatred, contempt, ridicule, or shame, or to discourage others from associating or dealing with him;

4. That one or more of the statements was false;

5. That the defendant failed to use reasonable care to determine the truth or falsity of one or more of the statement(s);

6. That the plaintiff suffered harm to his property, business, profession, or occupation, including money spent as a result of one or more of the statements; and

7. That one or more of the statements was a substantial factor in causing the plaintiff harm.

If the plaintiff has proved all of the above, then he is entitled to recover if he proves that the defendant's wrongful conduct was a substantial factor in causing any of the following actual damages:

a. Harm to the plaintiff's property, business, trade, profession, or occupation;

b. Expenses the plaintiff had to pay as a result of the defamatory statements;

c. Harm to the plaintiff's reputation; or

d. Shame, mortification, or hurt feelings.

Jury Instructions: Defamation

Slander Per Se

If the publication here injures the plaintiff in his office, trade, or business, the law presumes that the plaintiff has been damaged. The plaintiff does not have to allege or prove presumed damages. Those damages may include loss of customers or business, loss of contracts, or loss of employment.

You should consider from the evidence what award would be appropriate to compensate the injury to the reputation, shame, mortification, and hurt feelings. The plaintiff must still demonstrate some actual injury stemming from the defamatory statement(s), but the claim may be established at the minimum as a general claim of pain and suffering, such as embarrassment, humiliation, and temporary injury to reputation.

Punitive Damages

If in addition to your finding that the matter was published by communication to a third person, you may determine that the defendant acted with malice and may compensate the plaintiff. That award is called punitive damages. To recover for those damages, the plaintiff must prove by clear and convincing evidence that the defendant either knew the statements were false or had serious doubts about the truth of the statement, and that she acted with malice, oppression, or fraud.

Truth as a Defense

If you find that the defendant made one or more of the alleged defamatory statements and published them to a person or persons other than the plaintiff, then you must consider whether any and/or all of the statements was substantially true. Substantial truth is an absolute defense. Substantial truth does not require that every word be true. Substantial truth means that the substance of gist of a statement is true.

The burden is on the defendant to prove that any, if not all, of the statements were substantially true. If the defendant proves the truth of the statement, then it is an absolute defense and the verdict shall be for the defendant as to that particular statement made to a person or persons other than the plaintiff.

Conditional Privilege as a Defense

The defendant, Rita Slovin, has claimed that she had a qualified privilege to make one or more of the alleged defamatory statements to a person or persons other than the plaintiff. In order to show that a qualified privilege protects a certain statement, the defendant must show that:

1. the defendant had a good-faith reason to believe the statement was true;

2. the defendant had a personal or professional interest in knowing the information in the statement; and

3. the defendant shared the statement only with others who also had a personal or professional interest in knowing the information in the statement.

If the defendant reasonably believed that she was sharing information about a common interest and the listener(s) were entitled to know this, then the statement is protected as a matter of law.

The defendant also claims that she had made one or more of the alleged defamatory statements in response to a request and acted in good faith in making the statement. If you determine that the defendant has a qualified privilege, the plaintiff may still establish his claim, but only if the plaintiff convinces you that when the defendant made the statement she:

1. knew them to be false; or

2. spoke with a reckless disregard as to whether they were false; or

3. showed ill will toward the plaintiff; or

4. acted with a complete disregard of the plaintiff's rights; or

5. spoke in a way that shows insult or oppression.

Applicable Law: Battery

A person who intentionally touches another person without that person's consent and without justification is liable for any injury resulting from that intentional act.

Jury Instructions: Battery

1. **Elements of the Offense**. The plaintiff has alleged that the defendant assaulted and battered him, as set forth in his complaint. For you to find for the plaintiff, the plaintiff has to establish that the defendant, without the plaintiff's consent and without any justification, intentionally made physical contact with the plaintiff and, as a result of that contact, caused the plaintiff physical injury. A person is not justified in intentionally making physical contact with another person where the person making such contact is not in imminent danger of physical harm herself or for others. Physical injury is defined as an injury resulting in protracted impairment or substantial pain.

2. **Proximate Cause**. Here, the plaintiff claims that the defendant is liable for the plaintiff's psychic injuries, to wit, his emotional distress, stress, weight loss, and inability to sleep due to the suicide of his patient, and that the defendant should compensate the plaintiff for those injuries he suffered.

To establish that claim, the fact that a defendant's act caused injury is not, by itself, enough to impose legal responsibility on that defendant. Something more is needed. The party's improper conduct must be shown by a preponderance of the evidence to be a proximate cause of the physical or psychic injury claimed. A proximate cause brings about, or helps to bring about, the injury, and it must have been necessary to the result. For the defendant's act to be the proximate cause of the injury, it must both be an act but for which the harm would not have occurred and the injury has to be a foreseeable consequence of the act.

A foreseeable injury is one that an ordinary person, under the circumstances, would recognize or anticipate as creating a risk of injury. It is not necessary that the particular injury suffered was itself foreseeable, but only that the risk of that type of injury existed.

3. **Burden of Proof**. In this case, each party has a burden of proof. The burden of proof is the way our legal system decides who wins or loses a trial. The party who has the burden of proof cannot win unless you are convinced that each fact that the party must prove has been proven to a "preponderance of the evidence." "Preponderance of the evidence" means that based on all of the facts you have heard during the trial, you believe that each fact the party must prove is "more likely that not to be true." If you do not find that the fact is more likely than not to be true, the party with the burden of proof should not prevail.

4 **Circumstantial Evidence**. Evidence may be direct or circumstantial. Both direct and circumstantial evidence are sufficient to prove any element in this case. Direct evidence is simply the expression used to describe evidence that, by itself, if true, would establish a fact. Eyewitness testimony of a controverted fact is a clear example of direct evidence. Circumstantial evidence is such that although it does not directly prove a fact, it is the facts and circumstances that give rise to inferences about the controverted facts. If someone returned to their home and found a cookie jar broken in the middle of the kitchen floor, quickly checked the house and found nobody home but her young son, and then saw her young son with crumbs on his mouth, an inference could be drawn that the son broke the cookie jar.

5. **Credibility**. You are the sole judge of credibility of the witnesses. You are also the sole judge of how much weight to give to the testimony of any witnesses. In determining the credibility of a witness, you may consider her manner; appearance while testifying; any biases, prejudices, or incapacities that may have affected her judgment or truthfulness; and how her testimony compares to that of other witnesses whom you have found to be truthful, as well as any other factors that you deem appropriate.

PROBLEMS

COMPLETE TRIAL PROBLEMS

Child Custody—Bench Trial

Witnesses[1] for Rita Slovin (plaintiff):

Rita Slovin

Linda Allen

Serena Phillips (must be called to testify)

Witnesses for Michael Slovin (defendant):

Michael Slovin

Tommy Friel

Soren Elkind (must be called to testify)

Marital Tort (Battery)—Jury or Bench Trial on Liability Only

Witnesses for Michael Slovin (plaintiff):

Michael Slovin

Linda Allen

Witnesses for Rita Slovin (defendant):

Rita Slovin

Tommy Friel

Marital Tort (Defamation)—Jury or Bench Trial

Witnesses for Michael Slovin (plaintiff):

Michael Slovin

Anson Able

Witnesses for Rita Slovin (defendant):

Rita Slovin

Victoria Windsor

Equitable Distribution—Bench Trial

Witnesses[2] for Rita Slovin (plaintiff):

Rita Slovin

Tommy Friel

Rowena Marks (must be called to testify)

---

1. Witness Serena Phillips for the plaintiff (Rita Slovin) and witness Soren Elkind for the defendant (Michael Slovin) must be called to testify. For bench trials, however, each party must select one of the other witnesses to call. The remaining witness deposition will be deemed admitted by stipulation.
2. Witness Alan Brucker for the plaintiff (Michael Slovin) and witness Rowena Marks for the defendant (Rita Slovin) must be called to testify. For bench trials, however, each party must select one of the other witnesses to call. The remaining witness deposition will be deemed admitted by stipulation.

Witnesses for Michael Slovin (defendant):   Michael Slovin

Linda Allen

Alan Brucker (must be called to testify)

NEGOTIATION EXERCISES

Child Custody

Michael and Rita Slovin seek to resolve their dispute over custody.

- On behalf of Michael Slovin, represent him at a two-way negotiation of this matter.
- On behalf of Rita Slovin, represent her at a two-way negotiation of this matter.

Equitable Distribution

Michael and Rita Slovin seek to resolve their dispute over the division of the matrimonial property.

- On behalf of Michael Slovin, represent him at a "two-way"[3] negotiation of this matter.
- On behalf of Rita Slovin, represent her at a two-way negotiation of this matter.

All Issues: Custody, Equitable Distribution, Battery, Defamation

Michael and Rita Slovin seek to resolve all of the disputed matters (custody, equitable distribution, and the tort suit).

- On behalf of Michael Slovin, represent him at a two-way negotiation of these matters.
- On behalf of Rita Slovin, represent her at a two-way negotiation of these matters.

---

3. A "two-way" negotiation is one in which the attorneys negotiate without the presence of the parties.

WITNESS EXAMINATION PROBLEMS

Direct/Cross-Examination

Problem 1

Michael Slovin is testifying at the trial on his battery claim.

- On his behalf, conduct a direct and re-direct examination.
- On behalf of Rita Slovin, conduct a cross-examination.

Problem 2

Michael Slovin is testifying at the hearing on child custody.

- On his behalf, conduct a direct and re-direct examination.
- On behalf of Rita Slovin, conduct a cross-examination.

Problem 3

Rita Slovin is testifying at the trial on Michael Slovin's battery claim.

- On her behalf, conduct a direct and re-direct examination.
- On behalf of Michael Slovin, conduct a cross-examination.

Problem 4

Rita Slovin is testifying at the hearing on child custody.

- On her behalf, conduct a direct and re-direct examination.
- On behalf of Michael Slovin, conduct a cross-examination.

Problem 5

Michael Slovin is testifying at trial on his defamation claim.

- On his behalf, conduct a direct examination on the damages he allegedly sustained.
- On behalf of Rita Slovin, conduct a cross-examination.

Problem 6

Rita Slovin is testifying at trial on Michael Slovin's defamation claim.

- On her behalf, conduct a direct examination on her affirmative defenses.
- On behalf of Michael Slovin, conduct a cross-examination.

Problem 7

Tommy Friel is testifying at the trial on Michael Slovin's battery claim.

- On behalf of Rita Slovin, conduct a direct and re-direct examination.
- On behalf of Michael Slovin, conduct a cross-examination.

Problem 8

Tommy Friel is testifying at the hearing on the distribution of marital assets.

- On behalf of Rita Slovin, conduct a direct and re-direct examination.
- On behalf of Michael Slovin, conduct a cross-examination.

Problem 9

Linda Allen is testifying at the trial on Michael Slovin's battery claim.

- On behalf of Michael Slovin, conduct a direct and re-direct examination.
- On behalf of Rita Slovin, conduct a cross-examination.

Problem 10

Linda Allen is testifying at the hearing on child custody.

- On behalf of Michael Slovin, conduct a direct and re-direct examination.
- On behalf of Rita Slovin, conduct a cross-examination.

Impeachment

Problem 11

Linda Allen is testifying at a hearing on the child custody. On direct examination, she is asked the following question and gives the following answer.

Q: Prior to Michael and Rita's separation, what, if any, presents did Michael give you?

A: Before they were separated, he didn't give me any personal presents. He gave me a lovely necklace, however, as a Christmas present after the separation.

- On behalf of Rita Slovin, conduct a cross-examination.

Problem 12

Tommy Friel is testifying at a hearing on the distribution of marital assets. On cross- examination, he is asked the following question and gives the following answer.

Q: The company could not have grown after the death of the founder without the work of Rita Slovin, correct?

A: No. Her work was not a significant factor in the success of the company.

• On behalf of Michael Slovin, conduct a cross-examination on this issue.

Problem 13

Anson Able testifies on direct examination on Michael Slovin's defamation claim.

• On behalf of Rita Slovin, impeach Anson Able on the grounds of bias.

Problem 14

Victoria Windsor testifies on direct examination on Michael Slovin's defamation claim.

• On behalf of Michael Slovin, impeach Victoria Windsor on the grounds of bias.

Child Witness

Problem 15

Preparation of the child witness. Loren Slovin could be called by either parent on the battery claim or the custody issue.

• On the issue of the battery claim on behalf of Michael Slovin, explain the process of testifying to Loren Slovin and learn what she will say.

• On the issue of the battery claim on behalf of Rita Slovin, explain the process of testifying to Loren Slovin and learn what she will say.

Problem 16

Loren Slovin is called to testify on behalf of Michael Slovin at a hearing on her custody.

• On behalf of Michael Slovin, conduct a direct and re-direct examination.

• On behalf of Rita Slovin, conduct a cross-examination.

Problem 17

Loren Slovin is called to testify on behalf of Rita Slovin at a hearing on her custody.

- On behalf of Rita Slovin, conduct a direct and re-direct examination.
- On behalf of Michael Slovin, conduct a cross-examination.

Expert Witness

Problem 18

Dr. Serena Phillips is called to testify on behalf of Rita Slovin at a hearing on child custody.

- On behalf Rita Slovin, conduct a direct and re-direct examination.
- On behalf of Michael Slovin, conduct a cross-examination.

Problem 19

Soren Elkind is called to testify on behalf of Michael Slovin at a hearing on child custody.

- On behalf of Michael Slovin, conduct a direct and re-direct examination.
- On behalf of Rita Slovin, conduct a cross-examination.

Problem 20

Rowena Marks is called to testify on behalf of Rita Slovin at a hearing on the distribution of marital assets.

- On behalf Rita Slovin, conduct a direct and re-direct examination.
- On behalf of Michael Slovin, conduct a cross-examination.

Problem 21

Alan Brucker is called to testify on behalf of Michael Slovin at a hearing on the distribution of marital assets.

- On behalf of Michael Slovin, conduct a direct and re-direct examination.
- On behalf of Rita Slovin, conduct a cross-examination.

EXHIBITS

Exhibit 1

Hallway Diagram

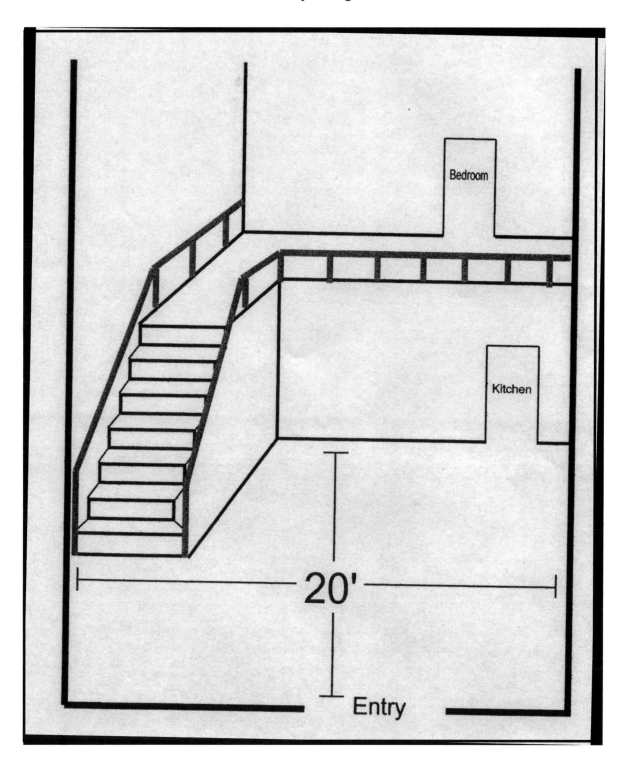

Exhibit 2

Floor Plan

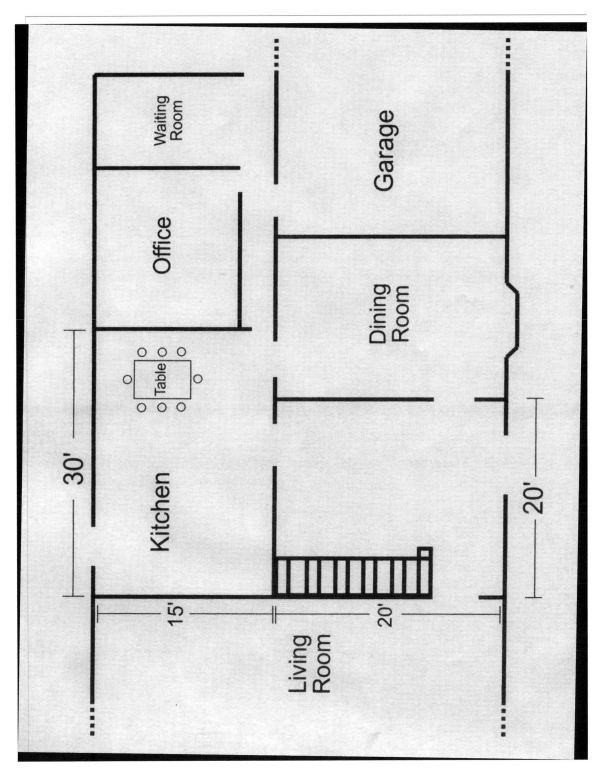

Exhibit 3

PERFECT TOYS, INCORPORATED
AGREEMENT
between

PERFECT TOYS, INCORPORATED ("Lender") *and* RITA SLOVIN ("Borrower")
DATE: 06/28/YR-8

WHEREAS RITA SLOVIN WISHES TO BORROW A CERTAIN SUM OF MONEY FROM PERFECT TOYS, INCORPORATED; AND
WHEREAS PERFECT TOYS, INCORPORATED HAS AGREED TO LEND RITA SLOVIN THAT MONEY; AND
WHEREAS RITA SLOVIN HAS AGREED TO REPAY THAT AMOUNT OF THE MONEY, THE FOLLOWING HAS BEEN AGREED TO:

As of the date of this Agreement, the Lender extends a line of credit in the amount of ONE MILLION DOLLARS ($1,000,000.00) at an annual rate of interest of ONE PER CENT (1 percent) to the Borrower. The line of credit has been established in the Perfect Toys In-House Special Account. The Borrower may draw from that line of credit at any time. The Borrower may repay any amount she draws from the line of credit at her convenience. The note must be repaid, in full, within 30 years from the this date, to wit, by 06/28/YR+22.

TERMS ARE AGREED TO AND ACKNOWLEDGED:

RITA SLOVIN   **PERFECT TOYS, INCORPORATED**
                            BY:

Exhibit 4

NATIONAL BANK OF NITA

NATIONAL BANK OF NITA, N.A. (BRANCH N-78)

P.O. BOX 5555

CITY ISLAND STATION,

NITA CITY, NITA 99999

RITA SLOVIN AND MICHAEL SLOVIN JTWOS   ACCOUNT : 444449870

670 MOCKINGBIRD SQUARE

NITA CITY, NITA 99907   AS OF 07/06/YR-8

YOUR MONEY IN THE BANK ACTIVITY FROM JUNE 7, YR-8 THROUGH JULY 6, YR-6

CHECKING PLUS

444449870

You began this statement period with a <u>BALANCE OF</u> $62,097.09

You increased funds as follows:

DEPOSITS

3/14/YR-6	$4,098.98
3/15/YR-6	1,000,000.00
3/28/YR-6	4,098.98

You decreased funds as follows:

Got cash from:

3/18/YR-6	#456	2,000.00
3/30/YR-6	#456	2,000.00

Checks paid

3/31/YR-6

Check # 970	1,000,000.00

You ended this statement period with a <u>BALANCE OF</u> $66,294.90

Exhibit 5

PERFECT TOYS, INCORPORATED

Statement of Revenues and Expenditures:
1/1/YR-11–12/31/YR-11

GROSS REVENUES

Sales	$9,120,000	
Commissions\fees\royalties	$460,000	
Contributions	N/A	
Investment income	$400,000	
Other revenues	$50,400	
Total revenues		$10,030,400

EXPENDITURES

Employee salaries	$5,500,000	
Commissions	$130,000	
Rent	$50,000	
Utilities	$10,000	
Materials	$2,300,000	
Office supplies	$30,000	
Advertising	$100,000	
Travel and entertainment	$35,000	
Professional services	$28,000	
Dues and subscriptions	$2,000	
Meetings and conferences	$10,000	
Communications	$40,000	
Insurance	$50,000	
Banking fees	$5,000	
Depreciation	$60,000	
Donations	$200,000	
Taxes	$200,000	
Other expenses	$11,000	
Total expenditures		$8,761,000

Net revenues $1,269,400

Exhibit 6

PERFECT TOYS, INCORPORATED

Statement of Revenues and Expenditures
1/1/YR-2 - 12/31/YR-2

REVENUES

Sales	$41,000,000	
Commissions \ fees \ royalties	$2,800,000	
Contributions	N/A	
Investment income	$400,000	
Other revenues	$1,000,400	
Total revenues		$45,200,400

EXPENDITURES

Employee salaries	$22,400,000	
Commissions	$200,000	
Rent	$920,000	
Utilities	$670,000	
Materials	$10,000,000	
Office supplies	$860,000	
Advertising	$1,800,000	
Travel and entertainment	$240,000	
Professional services	$100,000	
Dues and subscriptions	$35,000	
Meetings and conferences	$78,000	
Communications	$500,000	
Insurance	$1,800,000	
Banking fees	$70,000	
Depreciation	$900,000	
Donations	$1,200,000	
Taxes	$2,000,000	
Other expenses	$38,890	
Total expenditures		$43,811,890

Net revenues | | | **$1,388,510**

Exhibit 7

RITA SLOVIN
MICHEL SLOVIN

0970

Date 3/31/YR-6

Pay to the order of _M/M D. Ross_ $1,000,000.00

One million dollars and 00/100   Dollars

■ NATIONAL BANK OF NITA ■

Rita Slovin

memo _____

02■000089: 444449870" 0100   0970

Exhibit 8

NATIONAL BANK OF NITA

NATIONAL BANK OF NITA, N.A. (BRANCH N-78)
P.O. BOX 5555
CITY ISLAND STATION,
NITA CITY, NITA 99999

RITA SLOVIN AND MICHAEL SLOVIN JTWOS   ACCOUNT : 444449870
400 SCHOOLHOUSE LANE
NITA CITY, NITA 99907   AS OF 06/06/YR-2

YOUR MONEY IN THE BANK ACTIVITY FROM MAY 7, YR-2 THROUGH JUNE 6, YR-2

CHECKING PLUS
444449870

You began this statement period with a <u>BALANCE OF</u> $58,090.89

You increased funds as follows:

DEPOSITS
5/10/YR-2	$500.00
5/14/YR-2	$7,213.33
5/15/YR-2	$500.00
5/28/YR-2	$7,213.33
5/31/YR-2	$250.00

You decreased funds as follows:
Got cash from:
5/11/YR-2 #456	$400.00
5/16/YR-2 #456	$2,500.00
5/30/YR-2 #456	$2,500.00
6/02/YR-2 #456	$400.00

Checks paid
5/14/YR-2 Check #1970	$1,081.89
5/21/YR-2 Check #1971	$234.67
5/28/YR-2 Check #1972	$136.78
5/31/YR-2 Check# 1973	$246.98
5/31/YR-2 Check# 1974	$76.98
6/01/YR-2 Check# 1975	$45.09

You ended this statement period with a <u>BALANCE OF</u> $66,145.16

Exhibit 9

Beautiful Baubles

Jewelry for the discerning
14 Endicott Road
Nita City, Nita

12/12/YR-4
Sold to:

Michael Slovin - pickup/no address needed

Appraisal/insurance information

Diamond and ruby necklace set in 18 karat white gold
Twenty (20) diamond baguettes, weighing .25 carat each Quality : VS
One (1) full cut brilliant diamond, weighing 1.25 carats Quality : VVS
Twenty (20) ruby baguettes, weighing .15 carat each

Quantity	Ð scription	Price	Amount
1	diamond/ruby necklace	$5,500	5,500.00

Subtotal	5,500.00	
Tax Rate	7.00%	
Tax	385.00	
Freight	0.00	

TOTAL DUE $5,885.00 *PAID IN FULL*

We appreciate your business. Thank you!

Exhibit 10

NCMH

NITA COUNTY MEMORIAL HOSPITAL

EMERGENCY ROOM

PATIENT NAME: Michael Slovin

DATE OF BIRTH: 4/8/YR-38

DATE: December 19,YR-2

EMERGENCY ROOM PHYSICIAN: Green, M..

38-year-old male complains of pain in right forearm and swelling in elbow. Visual examination reveals low level cellulitis. No laceration or contusion noted.

Patient claims that his wife pushed him down the stairs of their residence three days prior to treatment. Patient drove himself to the emergency room.

Rx: Tylenol (over-the-counter-strength) as needed.
Ampillicin, 500 mg BID

Patient given the name and telephone number of ortho to consult if pain in elbow persists.

RELEASED FROM EMERGENCY ROOM: December 19, YR-2, 12:15hrs.

M. Green, M.D.

Exhibit 11

Bookerman Tennis
127 Smith Street
Nita, NITA

SCHEDULE

MEN'S "A" INDOOR LEAGUES
– Last Week in September - First Week in June

SINGLES:

Monday & Wednesday 3-5 P.M.

DOUBLES:

Tuesday & Thursday 3-5 P.M.

MEN'S "A" OUTDOOR LEAGUES

Second Week in June, Third Week in September

SINGLES:

Monday & Wednesday 3-5 P.M.

DOUBLES:

Tuesday & Thursday 3-5 P.M.

Exhibit 12

PERFECT TOYS, INCORPORATED
The World's Toy Center

100 TOYLAND AVENUE
NITA, NITA 45678

GEORGE HANOVER, PRESIDENT

December 1, YR-10

Dear Shareholders,

I am delighted to inform you that the recent sale of our aging manufacturing facilities has netted the company a $4 million profit. This permits me to make a one-time distribution of $1 million to each shareholder. This money will be distributed immediately. I have taken the liberty of creating a separate account for each shareholder. Your share of the distribution will be placed in this account and can be withdrawn by you at any time.

I expect that our new five-year plan will lead to a substantial increase in the profits of the company. I would, however, request that you make all efforts to invest the money that you withdraw from these accounts, conservatively. Since ours is a family business, I expect that I will be able to call on each of us to return the money if the company finds it necessary.

George Hanover
President

Exhibit 13

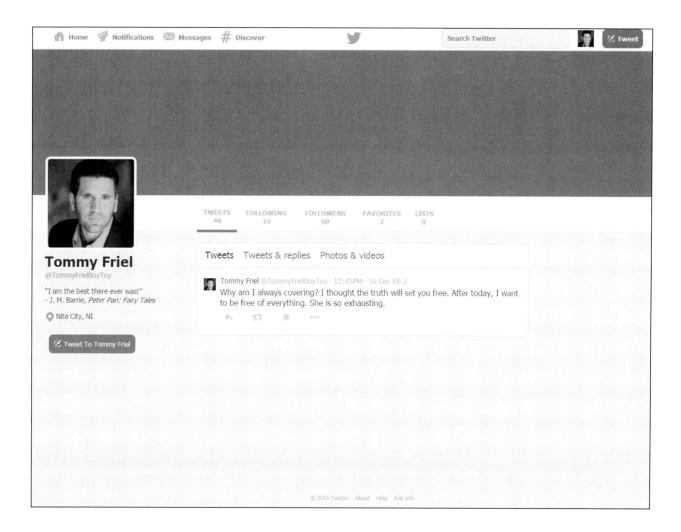

[*See* http://bit.ly/1bakDD0.]

Exhibit 14

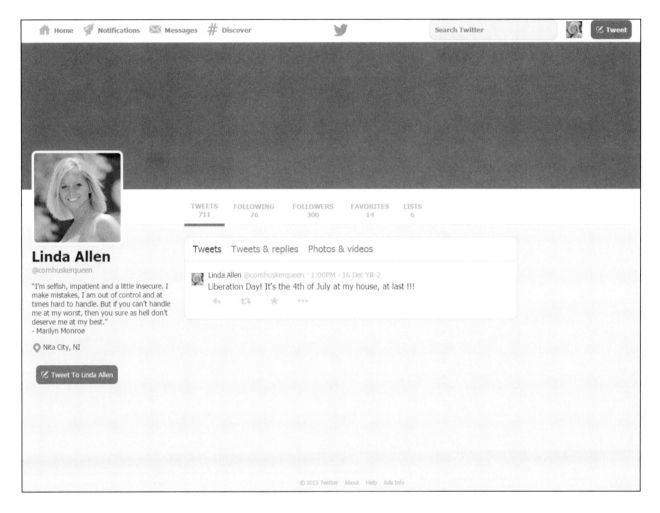

[*See* http://bit.ly/1GsUwjs.]